Aarti Sangrah

By Divinebharat

Art by Sujata Saha

ISBN 978-93-343-7113-0
Publisher: DivineBharat
Designer: Sujata Saha
Website: www.divinebharat.co

Index

II Vakratunda Mahakaya II

Vakratunda Mahakaya Suryakoti Samaprabha I
Nirvighnam Kuru Me Deva Sarvakaryeshu Sarvada II

II Jai Ganesh, Jai Ganesh II

Jai Ganesh Jai Ganesh, Jai Ganesh Deva I
Mata Jaki Parvati, Pita Mahadeva II
Ek Dant Dayavant, Char Bhuja Dhari I
Mathe Sindoor Sohe, Moose Ki Sawari II
Jai Ganesh Jai Ganesh, Jai Ganesh Deva I
Mata Jaki Parvati, Pita Mahadeva II
Paan Chadhe PhuChadhe, Aur Chadhe Mewa I
Ladduan Ka Bhog Lage, Sant Karen Seva II
Jai Ganesh Jai Ganesh, Jai Ganesh Deva I
Mata Jaki Parvati, Pita Mahadeva II
Andhan Ko Aankh Det, Kodhin Ko Kaya I
Baanjh Ko Putra Det, Nirdhan Ko Maya II
Jai Ganesh Jai Ganesh, Jai Ganesh Deva I
Mata Jaki Parvati, Pita Mahadeva II
Soor Shyam Sharan Aaye, Safal Kije Seva I
Jai Ganesh Jai Ganesh, Jai Ganesh Deva I
Mata Jaki Parvati, Pita Mahadeva II
Deenan Ki Laaj Rakho, Shambhu Sutkaari I
Kamna Ko Poorn Karo, Jaaun Balihari II
Jai Ganesh Jai Ganesh, Jai Ganesh Deva I
Mata Jaki Parvati, Pita Mahadeva II

II Ganpati ki seva mangal mewa II

Ganpati ki seva mangal mewa,
seva se sab vighn tarain I
Teen lok ke sakal devta,
dwar khade nit arj karain II
Ganpati ki seva mangal mewa...
Riddhi-siddhi dakshin-vam virajen,
aru anand son chamar karain
Dhoop-deep aru liye aarti,
bhakt khade jaykaar karain II
Ganpati ki seva mangal mewa...
Gud ke modak bhog lagat hain,
mooshak vahan chadhya sarain I
Saumya roop ko dekh Ganpati ke,
vighn bhag ja door parain II
Ganpati ki seva mangal mewa...
Bhado mas aru shukla chaturthi,
din dopara door parain I
Liyo janm Ganpati Prabhu ji,
Durga man anand bharain II
Ganpati ki seva mangal mewa...
Adbhut baja baja Indra ka,
dev bandhu sab gaan karain I
Shri Shankar ke anand upjya,
naam sunyo sab vighn tarain II

Ganpati ki seva mangal mewa...
Aani vidhata baithe aasan,
Indra-apsara nritya karain I
Dekh Ved-Brahma ji jako,
vighn vinashak naam dharain II
Ganpati ki seva mangal mewa...
Ekadant gajvadan Vinayak,
trinayan roop anup dharain I
Pagthambha sa udar pusht hai,
chandrama haasya karain II
Ganpati ki seva mangal mewa...
De shrap Shri Chandradev ko,
kalahīn tatkaal karain I
Chaudah lok mein phiren Ganpati,
teen lok mein raj karain II
Ganpati ki seva mangal mewa...
Uthi prabhat jap karain dhyan,
koi take karaj sarv sarain I
Pooja kaal aarti gaain,
take shir yash chhatra phirain II
Ganpati ki seva mangal mewa...
Ganpati ki pooja pehle karni,
kaam sabhi nirvighn sarain I
Sabhi bhakt Ganpati ji ke
haath jodkar stuti karain II

II Sukhakarta Dukhaharta II

Sukhakarta Dukhaharta Varta Vighnachi
Nuravi Purvi Prem Krupa Jayachi II
Sarvangi Sundar Uti Shendurachi I
Kanthi Jhalke Mal Muktaphalanchi II
Jai Dev Jai Dev, Jai Mangalmoorti I
Darshanmatre Mankamana Poorn Hoti II
II Jai Dev Jai Dev II

Ratnakhachit Phara Tuj Gaurikumara I
Chandanachi Uti Kunkumkeshara II
Hirejadit Mukut Shobhato Bara I
Runjhunati Nupure Charani Ghagariya II
II Jai Dev Jai Dev II

Lambodar Pitambar Phanivarbandhana I
Saral Son Vakratund Trinayana II
Das Ramacha Vaat Paahe Sadana I
Sankati Pavava Nirvani Rakshava II
II Jai Dev Jai Dev II

II Aarti Gazabdan Vinayak Ki II

Aarti Gazabdan Vinayak Ki I
Sur-muni-poojit Gananayak Ki II
Aarti Gazabdan Vinayak Ki II

Ekadant Shashibhaal Gajanan,
Vighnvinashak Shubhgun Kanan I
Shivasut Vandyamaan-Chaturanan,
Dukhvinashak Sukhdayak Ki II

Aarti Gazabdan Vinayak Ki II

Riddhi-Siddhi-Swami Samarth Ati,
Vimal Buddhi Data Suvimal-Mati I
Agh-Van-Dahan Amal Abhigat Gati,
Vidya-Vinay-Vibhav-Dayak Ki II

Aarti Gazabdan Vinayak Ki II

Pinglanayan, Vishal Shundadhar,
Dhoomravarn Shuchi Vajrankush-Kar I
Lambodar Badha-Vipatti-Har,
Sur-Vandit Sab Vidhi Layak Ki II

Aarti Gazabdan Vinayak Ki II

II Om Gan Ganapataye Namo Namah II

Shri Siddhivinayak Namo Namah
Ashtavinayak Namo Namah
Ganpati Bappa Morya
Om GanGanapataye Namo Namah

Shri Siddhivinayak Namo Namah
Ashtavinayak Namo Namah
Ganpati Bappa Morya
Om GanGanapataye Namo Namah

Shri Siddhivinayak Namo Namah
Ashtavinayak Namo Namah
Ganpati Bappa Morya
Om GanGanapataye Namo Namah

Shri Siddhivinayak Namo Namah
Ashtavinayak Namo Namah
Ganpati Bappa Morya

II Maha Ganapatim Manasa Smarami II

Maha Ganapatim Manasa Smarami
Vinayakavibhum Vatapatrasinam
Mahakavinutam Mahadevam
Madhuraswarapriyataram Sandeham

Mandardharam Sandarshita Premaṃ
Mudakaram Chandrardhamaulisutam
Sindooravarṇam Sindhruvahanam
Sindoorasundaravigraham Gambhiram

Amarasaptaswaravinutam
Aganitamahimam Asuranikandanam
Samarasavarṇam Satatam
Yogijanaservitam Santatam
Suramuniganánutam

Namrataram Natyavinodamodam
Navarasagaanamuditahridayam
Nadasvarapriya
Nanavidhaparishadanutam
Natakadisampreerakam

II Gananayakaya Ganadaivataya II

Gananayakaya Ganadaivataya
Ganadhyakshaya Dhimahi
Gunashriraya Gunamanditaya
Guneshanaya Dhimahi
Gunatitaya Gunadhishaya
Gunapravishtaya Dhimahi
Ekadantaya Vakratundaya
Gauritanayaya Dhimahi
Gajeshanaya Balachandraya
Shriganesaya Dhimahi
Ekadantaya Vakratundaya
Gauritanayaya Dhimahi
Gajeshanaya Balachandraya
Shriganesaya Dhimahi
Ganachaturaya Ganapranaya
Ganantaratmane
Ganotsukaya Ganamattaya
Ganotsuka Manase
Gurpujitaya Gurudaivataya
Gurukulasthayine
Guruvikramaya Guhyapravaraya
Gurave Gunagurave
Gurudaitya Kalakshetre
Gurudharma Sadaradhyaya
Guruputra Paritratre
Gurupakhanda Khandakaya
Geetasaraya Geetatattvaya
Geetagotraya Dhimahi
Gudhagulfaya Gandhamattaya
Gojayapradaya Dhimahi
Gunatitaya Gunadhishaya
Gunapravishtaya Dhimahi
Ekadantaya Vakratundaya
Gauritanayaya Dhimahi
Gajeshanaya Balachandraya

Shriganesaya Dhimahi
Ekadantaya Vakratundaya
Gauritanayaya Dhimahi
Gajeshanaya Balachandraya
Shriganesaya Dhimahi
Sarvarajaya Gandhanam
Sarvaganashravanapranayine
Gadhaya Ragaya Granthaya
Gitaya Granthartha Tanamayine
Gurilaye Gunavate Ganapataye
Granthagitaya Granthageyaya
Granthantraratmane
Gitalinaya Gitashrayaya Gitvadya
Pataye
Dhyeyacharitaya Gayakavaraya
Gandharvapriyakrpe
Gayakadhina Vigrahaya
Gangajal Pranayavate
Gauristanandhanaya
Gaurahridaya Nandanaya
Gaurabhanusutaya
Gauriganeshvaraya
Gaurapranayaya Gauripravanaya
Gaurabhavaya Dhimahi
Ghoshasastraya Govardhanaya
Gopagopaya Dhimahi
Gunatitaya Gunadhishaya
Gunapravishtaya Dhimahi
Ekadantaya Vakratundaya
Gauritanayaya Dhimahi
Gajeshanaya Balachandraya
Shriganesaya Dhimahi
Ekadantaya Vakratundaya
Gauritanayaya Dhimahi
Gajeshanaya Balachandraya
Shriganesaya Dhimahi

II Om Tryambakam Yajamahe II

Om Tryambakam Yajamahe
Sugandhim Pushtivardhanam I
Urvarukamiva Bandhanan
Mrityormukshiya Mamritat II

Karpoora Gauram Karunavataram
Samsarasaram Bhujagendraharam I
Sada Basantam Hridayarabinde
Bhavam Bhavanisahitam Namami II

II Ashutosh Shashank Shekhar II

Ashutosh Shashank Shekhar,
Chandra Mauli Chidambara,
Koti Koti Pranam Shambhu,
Koti Naman Digambara I I

Nirvikar Omkar Avinashi, Tumhi Devadhi Dev,
Jagat Sarjak Pralay Karta,
Shivam Satyam Sundara I I

Nirankar Swaroop Kaleshwar, Maha Yogishwara,
Dayanidhi Danishwar Jai,
Jatadhar Abhayankara I I

Shool Pani Trishool Dhari, Augdi Baghambari,
Jai Mahesh Trilochanaya,
Vishwanath Vishambara I I

Nath Nageshwar Haro Har,
Pap Saap Abhishap Tam,
Mahadev Mahan Bhole, Sada Shiv Shiv Sankara I I

Jagat Pati Anurakati Bhakti,
Sadaiv Tere Charan Ho,
Kshama Ho Aparadh Sab,
Jai Jayati Jagadishwara I I

Janam Jeevan Jagat Ka, Santap Taap Mite Sabhi,
Om Namah Shivaya Man,
Japta Rahe Panchakshara I I

Ashutosh Shashank Shekhar,
Chandra Mauli Chidambara,
Koti Koti Pranam Shambhu,
Koti Naman Digambara I I

II Om Namah Shivaya II

Om Namah Shivaya,
Om Namah Shivaya
Har Har Bhole Namah Shivaya,
Om Namah Shivaya,
Om Namah Shivaya,
Har Har Bhole Namah Shivaya....
Rameshwaraya, Shiv, Rameshwaraya,
Har Har Bhole Namah Shivaya,
Rameshwaraya, Shiv, Rameshwaraya,
Har Har Bhole Namah Shivaya....
Gangadharaya, Shiv, Gangadharaya,
Har Har Bhole Namah Shivaya,
Gangadharaya, Shiv, Gangadharaya,
Har Har Bhole Namah Shivaya....
Jatadharaya, Shiv, Jatadharaya,
Har Har Bhole Namah Shivaya,
Jatadharaya, Shiv, Jatadharaya,
Har Har Bhole Namah Shivaya....
Someshwaraya, Shiv, Someshwaraya,
Har Har Bhole Namah Shivaya,

Someshwaraya, Shiv, Someshwaraya,
Har Har Bhole Namah Shivaya….
Vishweshwaraya, Shiv, Vishweshwaraya,
Har Har Bhole Namah Shivaya,
Vishweshwaraya, Shiv, Vishweshwaraya,
Har Har Bhole Namah Shivaya….
Koteshwaraya, Shiv, Koteshwaraya,
Har Har Bhole Namah Shivaya,
Koteshwaraya, Shiv, Koteshwaraya,
Har Har Bhole Namah Shivaya….
Mahakaleshwaraya,
Mahakaleshwaraya,
Har Har Bhole Namah Shivaya,
Mahakaleshwaraya,
Mahakaleshwaraya,
Har Har Bhole Namah Shivaya….
Tryambakeshwaraya, Shiv,
Tryambakeshwaraya,
Har Har Bhole Namah Shivaya,
Tryambakeshwaraya, Shiv,
Tryambakeshwaraya,
Har Har Bhole Namah Shivaya….

Bhadreshwaraya, Shiv,
Bhadreshwaraya,
Har Har Bhole Namah Shivaya,
Bhadreshwaraya, Shiv,
Bhadreshwaraya,
Har Har Bhole Namah Shivaya....
Yogeshwaraya, Shiv, Yogeshwaraya,
Har Har Bhole Namah Shivaya,
Yogeshwaraya, Shiv, Yogeshwaraya,
Har Har Bhole Namah Shivaya....
Mamaleshwaraya, Shiv,
Mamaleshwaraya,
Har Har Bhole Namah Shivaya,
Mamaleshwaraya, Shiv,
Mamaleshwaraya,
Har Har Bhole Namah Shivaya....
Bhimeshwaraya, Shiv,
Bhimeshwaraya,
Har Har Bhole Namah Shivaya,
Bhimeshwaraya, Shiv,
Bhimeshwaraya,
Har Har Bhole Namah Shivaya....

Gangeshwaraya, Shiv,
Gangeshwaraya,
Har Har Bhole Namah Shivaya,
Gangeshwaraya, Shiv,
Gangeshwaraya,
Har Har Bhole Namah Shivaya....
Kameshwaraya, Shiv, Kameshwaraya,
Har Har Bhole Namah Shivaya,
Kameshwaraya, Shiv, Kameshwaraya,
Har Har Bhole Namah Shivaya....
Rudreshwaraya, Shiv, Rudreshwaraya,
Har Har Bhole Namah Shivaya,
Rudreshwaraya, Shiv, Rudreshwaraya,
Har Har Bhole Namah Shivaya....
Om Namah Shivaya
Om Namah Shivaya,
Har Har Bhole Namah Shivaya,
Om Namah Shivaya,
Om Namah Shivaya,
Har Har Bhole Namah Shivaya II

II Om Jai Shiv Omkara II

Om Jai Shiv Omkara,
Prabhu Jai Shiv Omkara I
Brahma, Vishnu, Sadashiva,
Ardhangi Dhara II
Om Jai Shiv Omkara...

Ekanan Chaturanan
Panchanan Raje I
Hansasan Garudasana
Vrishvahan Saje
Om Jai Shiv Omkara...

Do Bhuj Char Chaturbhuj
Das Bhuj Tejdhari I
Trigun Swaroop Nirakhat
Tribhuvan Jan Nari II
Om Jai Shiv Omkara...

Akshmala Vanmala
Mundmala Dhari I
Chandan Mrigmad Sohe
Bhal Shubh Bichari II
Om Jai Shiv Omkara...

Shwetambar Peetambar
Baghambar Ange I
Sankat Mochan Swami
Bhaktan Ke Sange II
Om Jai Shiv Omkara...

Kar Ke Madhya Kamandalu
Chakra Trishuldhari I
Sukhakarta Dukhaharta
Tribhuvan Bhartari II
Om Jai Shiv Omkara...

Bhasmalankar Kiye
Bhooton Ke Swami
Tripurari Jagpalak
Shankar Bhavbhami
Om Jai Shiv Omkara...

Srishti Ke Palankarta
Jag Ke Vidhata I
Kripa Karo He Shankar
Palan Karo Natha II
Om Jai Shiv Omkara...

II Har Har Har Mahadev II

Har Har Har Mahadev!
Satya, Sanatan, Sundar,
Shiv Sabke Swami I
Avikari Avinashi, Aj Antaryami II
Har Har Har Mahadev!
Aadi, Anant, Anamay, Akal, Kaladhari I
Amal, Arup, Agochar, Avichal,
Aghahari II
Har Har Har Mahadev!
Brahma, Vishnu, Maheshwar
Tum Trimurtidhari I
Karta, Bharta, Dharta, Tum Hi
Sanhari II
Har Har Har Mahadev!
Rakshak, Bhakshak, Prerak,
Priya Audhardani I
Sakshi, Param Akarta,
Karta Abhimani II
Har Har Har Mahadev!
Manimay-Bhavan Nivasi,
Ati Bhogi Ragi I
Sada Shmashan Vihari, Yogi Vairagi II
Har Har Har Mahadev!
Chhal-Kapal, Garal-Gal,
Mundmal Vyaali I

Chita Bhasmatan Trinayan,
Ayanmahakali II
Har Har Har Mahadev!
Pret-Pishach-Susevit, Peet Jatadhari I
Vivasan Vikat Rupadhar,
Rudra Pralaykari II
Har Har Har Mahadev!
Shubhra-Saumya, Sursaridhar,
Shashidhar, Sukhkari I
Atikamaniya, Shantikaar, Shivmuni
Man-Hari II
Har Har Har Mahadev!
Nirgun, Sagun, Niranjan,
Jagmay Nitya Prabho I
Kalarup Keval Har! Kalatit Vibho II
Har Har Har Mahadev!
Sat, Chit, Anand, Rasamay,
Karunamay Dhata I
Prem-Sudha-Nidhi Priyatam,
Akhil Vishv Trata II
Har Har Har Mahadev!
Hum Atideen, Dayamay!
Charan-Sharan Deeje I
Sab Vidhi Nirmal Mati Kar,
Apna Kar Leeje II
Har Har Har Mahadev!

II Kaal ki Vikarl ki II

Kaal ki Vikarl ki
Trilokeshwar Trikal ki
Bhole Shiv Kripal ki
Karo re Mangal Aarti
Mrityunjay Mahakal ki

Baba Mahakal ki
O mere Mahakal ki
Karo re Mangal Aarti
Mrityunjay Mahakal ki

Pit Pushp Baghambar Dhari
Nandi teri Sawari
Tripunddhari he Tripurari
Bhole Bhav Bhayahari
Shambhu din dayal ki
teen lok digpal ki
Kailashi Shashibhal ki
Karo re Mangal Aarti
Mrityunjay Mahakal ki

Damru baje
dam dam dam dam
Nache Shankar Bhola

Bam Bhole Shiv
bam bam bam bam
Chadha bhang ka gola
Jai jai hriday vishal ki
Ashutosh pratipal ki
Nauna dhak dhak jyala ki
Karo re Mangal Aarti
Mrityunjay Mahakal ki

Aarat hari palanhari
tu hai mangalkari
Aarat hari palanhari
tu hai mangalkari
Mangal Aarti kare nar nari
paaye padarath chari
Kalarup Mahakal ki
kripasindhu Mahakal ki
Ujjaini Mahakal ki
Karo re Mangal Aarti
Mrityunjay Mahakal ki

Baba Mahakal ki
o mere Mahakal ki
Karo re Mangal Aarti
Mrityunjay Mahakal ki

II Om Jai Gangadhar Jai Har II

Om Jai Gangadhar Jai Har,
Jai Girijadhisha I
Tvam Mam Palaya Nityam,
Kripaya Jagadisha II
Om Har Har Har Mahadev II
Kailase Girishikhare,
Kalpadrumavipine I
Gunjati Madhukarapunje,
Kunjavane Gahane II
Om Har Har Har Mahadev II
Kokilakoojit Khelat, Hansavan Lalita I
Rachayati Kalakalapam,
Nrityati Mudasahita II
Om Har Har Har Mahadev II
Tasmin Lalitasudeshe,
Shala Manirachita I
Tanmadhye Harnikate,
Gauri Mudasahita I
Krida Rachayati,
Bhusharanchit Nijmisham I
Indradik Sur Sevat,
Namayate Sheesham II
Om Har Har Har Mahadev II
Bibudhabadhu Bahu Nrityat,
Hridaye Mudasahita I
Kinnar Gayan Kurute,

Sapt Swar Sahita II
Dhinkat Thai Thai Dhinkat,
Mridang Vadayate I
Kvan Kvan Lalita Venum,
Madhuram Natayate II
Om Har Har Har Mahadev II
Run Run Charane Rachayati,
Nupurumujjvalita I
Chakravarte Bhramayati,
Kurute Tam Dhik Tam II
Om Har Har Har Mahadev II
Tam Tam Lup Chup,
Tam Tam Damru Vadayate I
Angusthangulinadam,
Laskatan Kurute II
Om Har Har Har Mahadev II
Kapurradyutigauram,
Panchananasahitam I
Trinayan Shashidhar Maulin,
Vishadhara Kanthayutam II
Om Har Har Har Mahadev II
Sundarjatayakalapam,
Pavakayutabhalam I
Damrutrishulapinakam,
Karadhrit Nrikapalam II
Om Har Har Har Mahadev II
Mundai Rachayati Mala,
Pannagamupavitam I

Vamavibhage Girija,
Roopam Atilalitam II
Om Har Har Har Mahadev II
Sundarasakalasharire,
Kritabhasmabharanam I
Iti Vrishabhadhwajarupam,
Tapatrayaharanam II
Om Har Har Har Mahadev II
Shankhaninadham Kritva,
Jhallari Nadayate I
Nirajayate Brahma,
Vedricham Pathate II
Om Har Har Har Mahadev II
Atimridu Charanasarojam,
Hritkamale Dhrtva I
Avalokayati Mahesham,
Isham Abhinatva II
Om Har Har Har Mahadev II
Dhyanam Aarti Samaye,
Hridaye Ati Kritva I
Ramastrijatanatham,
Isham Abhinatva II
Om Har Har Har Mahadev II
Sangatimevam Pratidin,
Pathanam Yah Kurute I
Shivasayujyam Gachchhati,
Bhaktya Yah Shrnute II
Om Har Har Har Mahadev II

II Jayati Jayati Jag-Nivas II

Jayati Jayati Jag-Nivas,
Shankar Sukhkari II

Jayati Jayati Jag-Nivas,
Shankar Sukhkari II

Jayati Jayati Jag-Nivas... II

Ajar Amar Aj Arup,
Sat Chit Anandrup I

Vyapak Brahmaswaroop,
Bhav! Bhav-Bhay-Hari II

Jayati Jayati Jag-Nivas... II

Shobhit Bidhubal Bhal,
Sursarimay Jatajal I

Teen Nayan Ati Vishal,
Madan-Dahan-Kari II

Jayati Jayati Jag-Nivas... II

Bhakthetu Dharat Shool,
Karat Kathin Shool Phool I

Hiyki Sab Harat Hul Achal Shantikari II

Jayati Jayati Jag-Nivas... II

Amal Arun Charan Kamal
saphal Karat Kamasakal I

Bhakti-Mukti Det Vimal,
Maya-Bhram-Tari II

Jayati Jayati Jag-Nivas... II

Kartikeyayut Ganesh,
Himtanaya Sah Mahesh I

Rajat Kailas-Desh, Akal Kaladhari II

Jayati Jayati Jag-Nivas... II

Bhushan Tan Bhuti Byal,
Mundamal Kar Kapal I
Sinh-Charm Hasti Khal,
Damru Kar Dhari II

Jayati Jayati Jag-Nivas... II

Asharan Jan Nitya Sharan,
Ashutosh Aartiharan I
Sab Vidhi Kalyan-Karan
Jay Jay Tripurari II

Jayati Jayati Jag-Nivas... II

II Sheesh Gang Ardhang Parvati II

Sheesh Gang Ardhang Parvati,
Sada Virajat Kailasi.
Nandi Bhringi Nritya Karat Hain,
Dharat Dhyan Sur Sukharasi II

Sheetal Mand Sugandh Pawan,
Bah Baithe Hain Shiv Avinashi.
Karat Gaan-Gandharv Sapt Swar,
Raag Ragini Madhurasi II

Yaksha-Raksh-Bhairav Jahan Dolat,
Bolat Hain Vanake Vasi.
Koyal Shabd Sunavat Sundar,
Bhramar Karat Hain Gunja-si II

Kalpadrum Aru Parijat Taru,
Laag Rahe Hain Lakshasi.
Kamdhenu Kotin Jahan Dolat,
Karat Dugdh Ki Varsha-si II

Suryakant Sam Parvat Shobhit,
Chandrakant Sam Himrashi.
Nitya Chahoon Ritu Rahat Sushobhit,
Sevat Sada Prakriti Dasi II

Rishi Muni Dev Danuj Nit Sevat,
Gaan Karat Shruti Gunrashi.

Brahma, Vishnu Niharata Nisidin,
Kachu Shiv Hamkoon Farmasi II

Riddhi-Siddhi Ke Data Shankar,
Nit Sat Chit Aanandrashi.
Jinke Sumirat Hi Kat Jati,
Kathin Kaal Yamki Phansi II

Trishuldharji Ka Naam Nirantar,
Prem Sahit Jo Nar Gasi.
Door Hoy Vipda Us Nar Ki,
Janm-Janm Shivpad Pasi II

Kailasi Kashi Ke Vasi,
Vinashi Meri Sudh Leejo.
Sevak Jaan Sada Charanan Ko,
Apno Jaan Kripa Keejo II

Tum To Prabhuji Sada Dayamay,
Avagun Mere Sab Dhakiyo.
Sab Aparadh Kshamakar Shankar,
Kinkar Ki Vinati Suniyo II

Sheesh Gang Ardhang Parvati,
Sada Virajat Kailasi.
Nandi Bhringi Nritya Karat Hain,
Dharat Dhyan Sur Sukharasi II

II Om Jai Jagdish Hare II

Om Jai Jagdish Hare,
Swami! Jai Jagdish Hare I
Bhakt Jano Ke Sankat,
Kshan Mein Door Kare II
Om Jai Jagdish Hare I
Jo Dhyaave Phal Paave,
Dukh Vinase Man Ka I
Swami Dukh Vinase Man Ka I
Sukh Sampatti Ghar Aave,
Kasht Mite Tan Ka II
Om Jai Jagdish Hare I
Maat-Pita Tum Mere,
Sharan Gahun Main Kiski I
Swami Sharan Gahun Main Kiski I
Tum Bin Aur Na Dooja, Aas Karun Jiski II
Om Jai Jagdish Hare I
Tum Poorn Paramatma, Tum Antaryami I
Swami Tum Antaryami I
Parabrahm Parameshwar,
Tum Sabke Swami II
Om Jai Jagdish Hare I
Tum Karuna Ke Saagar, Tum Palan-Karta I

Swami Tum Palan-Karta I
Main Moorakh Khal Kaami,
Kripa Karo Bharta II
Om Jai Jagdish Hare I
Tum Ho Ek Agochar, Sabke Pranpati I
Swami Sabke Pranpati I
Kis Vidhi Miloon Dayamay,
Tumko Main Kumati II
Om Jai Jagdish Hare I
Deenbandhu Dukh Harta,
Tum Thakur Mere I
Swami Tum Thakur Mere I
Apne Haath Uthao, Dwar Pada Tere II
Om Jai Jagdish Hare I
Vishay-Vikaar Mitao, Paap Haro Deva I
Swami Paap Haro Deva I
Shraddha-Bhakti Badhao, Santan Ki Seva II
Om Jai Jagdish Hare I
Shri Jagdishji Ki Aarti, Jo Koi Nar Gave I
Swami Jo Koi Nar Gave I
Kahat Shivanand Swami,
Sukh Sampatti Pave II
Om Jai Jagdish Hare I

II Jai Lakshmi Ramana II

Jai Lakshmi Ramana
Shri Jai Lakshmi Ramana I
Satyanarayan Swami
Janapatak Harana II

Jai Lakshmi Ramana I

Ratna Jadit Simhasan
Adbhut Chhavi Raje I
Narad Karat Nirajan
Ghanta Dhvani Baje II

Jai Lakshmi Ramana I

Pragat Bhaye Kali Karan
Dvija Ko Darsh Diyo I
Boodho Brahman Bankar
Kanchan Mahal Kiyo II

Jai Lakshmi Ramana I

Durbal Bhil Katharo In Par Kripa Kari I
Chandrachood Ek Raja
Jinki Vipati Hari II

Jai Lakshmi Ramana I

Vaishya Manorath Payo
Shraddha Taj Dini I

So Phal Bhogyo Prabhuji
Phir Stuti Kini II

Jai Lakshmi Ramana I

Bhav Bhakti Ke Karan
Chin-Chin Roop Dharyo I
Shraddha Dharan Kini
Tinko Kaaj Saryo II

Jai Lakshmi Ramana I

Gwal Bal Sang Raja
Van Mein Bhakti Kari I
Manvanchit Phal Dino
Deendayal Hari II

Jai Lakshmi Ramana I

Chadhat Prasad Savaya
Kadali Phal Mewa I
Dhoop Deep Tulsi Se Raji Satyadeva II

Jai Lakshmi Ramana I

Shri Satyanarayanji Ki Aarti
Jo Koi Nar Gave I
Kahat Shivanand Swami
Manvanchit Phal Pave II

Jai Lakshmi Ramana I

II Jai Purushottam Deva II

Jai Purushottam Deva
Sab maason mein uttam, tumko batlaya.
Kripa hui jab Hari ki, Krishna roop paya.
Jai Purushottam Deva
Pooja tumko jisne, sarv sukh deena.
Nirmal karke kaya, paap chhaar keena.
Jai Purushottam Deva
Medhavi muni kanya, mahima jab jani.
Droupadi naam sati se, jag ne sanmani.
Jai Purushottam Deva
Vipra Sudev seva kar,
mrut sut puni paya.
Dham Hari ka paya,
yash jag mein chhaya.
Jai Purushottam Deva
Nrip Dridhdhanva par jab,
tumne kripa kari.
Vratvidhi niyam aur pooja,
keeni bhakti bhari.
Jai Purushottam Deva
Shudra Manigriv paapi, deepdan kiya.
Nirmal buddhi tum karke,
Hari dham diya.
Jai Purushottam Deva
Purushottam vrat-poojahit chit se karte.
Prabhudas bhav nad se, sahaj hi ve tarte.
Jai Purushottam Deva

II Shriman Narayan Narayan Hari Hari II

Shriman Narayan Narayan Hari Hari
Tava Mahima Anant, Ati Pyari Hari Hari
Lakshmi Narayan Narayan Hari Hari
Charan Sharan Mein Bhakti Hamari
Hari Hari
Bhajo Man Narayan Narayan Hari Hari
Jai Jai Narayan Narayan Hari Hari
Satya Narayan Narayan Hari Hari
Dukhahari, Sukhkari Hari Hari
Hari Om Namo Narayan Hari Hari
Shuddh Naam Amrit Saar Hari Hari
Govind Narayan Narayan Hari Hari
Vishnu Narayan Narayan Hari Hari
Bhajo Man Narayan Narayan Hari Hari
Jai Jai Narayan Narayan Hari Hari
Badrinarayan Narayan Hari Hari
Jagannath Narayan Narayan Hari Hari
Patit Pawan, Prabhu Kripalu Hari Hari
Hari Om Namo Narayan Hari Hari
Tava Leela Sabse Nyari Nyari Hari HariII

ll Om Jai Narsingh Hare ll

Om Jai Narsingh Hare,
Prabhu Jai Narsingh Hare
Stambh Fad Prabhu Prakate,
Stambh Fad Prabhu Prakate
Jan Ka Taap Hare
Om Jai Narsingh Hare
Tum Ho Deen Dayala,
Bhaktan Hitkari,
Prabhu Bhaktan Hitkari
Adbhut Roop Banakar,
Adbhut Roop Banakar
Prakate Bhay Hari
Om Jai Narsingh Hare
Sabke Hriday Vidaran,
Dusyu Jiyo Mari,
Prabhu Dusyu Jiyo Mari
Das Jaan Apnayo, Das Jaan Apnayo
Jan Par Kripa Kari
Om Jai Narsingh Hare
Brahma Karat Aarti,
Mala Pehinave,
Prabhu Mala Pehinave
Shivji Jai Jai Kahkar,
Pushpan Barasave
Om Jai Narsingh Hare

II Aarti Kijai Narasimha Kunwar Ki II

Aarti Kijai Narasimha Kunwar Ki
Ved Vimal Yash Gaun Mere Prabhuji

Pehli Aarti Prahlad Ubare
Hiranakush Nakh Udar Vidare

Doosri Aarti Vaman Seva
Bali Ke Dwar Padhare Hari Deva

Teesri Aarti Brahma Padhare
Sahasbahu Ke Bhujha Ukhare

Chauthi Aarti Asur Sanhare
Bhakt Vibhishan Lanka Padhare

Paanchvi Aarti Kans Pachhare
Gopi Gwal Sakha Pratipale

Tulsi Ko Patra Kanth Mani Heera
Harshi-Nirakhi Gaaven Das Kabira

II Aarti Kunjbihari Ki II

Aarti Kunjbihari Ki,
Shri Giridhar Krishna Murari Ki
Gale Mein Baijanti Mala,
Bajave Murli Madhur Bala I

Shravan Mein Kundal Jhalakala,
Nand Ke Anand Nandlala I

Gagan Sam Ang Kanti Kali,
Radhika Chamak Rahi Aali I

Latan Mein Thadhe Banmali;
Bhramar Si Alak, Kasturi Tilak,
Chandra Si Jhalak;
Lalit Chhavi Shyama Pyari Ki II

Shri Giridhar Krishnamurari Ki II

Aarti Kunjbihari Ki
Shri Giridhar Krishna Murari Ki

Kankamay Mor Mukut Bilasai,
Devta Darshan Ko Tarsai I

Gagan So Suman Rasi Barsai;
Baje Murchang, Madhur Miradang,
Gwalin Sang;
Atul Rati Gop Kumari Ki II

Shri Giridhar Krishnamurari Ki II

Aarti Kunjbihari Ki Shri Giridhar
Krishna Murari Ki
Jahan Te Prakat Bhai Ganga,
Kalush Kali Harini Shriganga I
Smaran Te Hot Moh Bhanga;
Basi Siv Sis, Jata Ke Beech,
Hare Agh Keech;
Charan Chhavi Shribanwari Ki II

Shri Giridhar Krishnamurari Ki II

Aarti Kunjbihari Ki Shri Giridhar
Krishna Murari Ki

Chamakti Ujjval Tat Renu,
Baj Rahi Vrindavan Benu I
Chahun Disi Gopi Gwal Dhenu;
Hansat Mridu Mand, Chandani Chand,
Katat Bhav Fand;
Ter Sun Din Bikhari Ki II

Shri Giridhar Krishnamurari Ki II

Aarti Kunjbihari Ki Shri Giridhar
Krishna Murari Ki

II Shri Bankebihari teri aarti gaaun II

Kunjbihari teri aarti gaaun I
Shri Shyamsundar teri aarti gaaun I
Shri Bankebihari teri aarti gaaun II
Mor mukut prabhu sheesh pe sohe I
Pyari banshi mero man mohe I
Dekhi chhavi balihaari jaaun I
Shri Bankebihari teri aarti gaaun II
Charanon se nikli ganga pyari I
Jisne saari duniya taari I
Main un charanon ke darshan paun I
Shri Bankebihari teri aarti gaaun II
Daas anath ke naath aap ho I
Dukh sukh jeevan pyare saath ho I
Hari charanon mein sheesh navaun I
Shri Bankebihari teri aarti gaaun II
Shri Hari daas ke pyare tum ho I
Mere Mohan jeevan dhan ho I
Dekhi yugal chhavi bali-bali jaaun I
Shri Bankebihari teri aarti gaaun II
Aarti gaaun pyare tumko rijhaun I
He Giridhar teri aarti gaaun I
Shri Shyamsundar teri aarti gaaun I
Shri Bankebihari teri aarti gaaun II

II Aarti Shri Govardhan Maharaj Ki II

Shri Govardhan Maharaj, o Maharaj,
Tere maathe mukut viraj raheo I
Tope paan chadhe tope phool chadhe,
Tope chadhe doodh ki dhaar I
Tere maathe mukut viraj raheo I
Teri saat kos ki parikkamma,
Chakleshwar hai vishraam I
Tere maathe mukut viraj raheo I
Tere gale mein kantha saaj raheo,
Thodi pe heera laal I
Tere maathe mukut viraj raheo I
Tere kaanan kundal chamak raheo,
Teri jhaanki bani vishaal I
Tere maathe mukut viraj raheo I
Giriraj dharan prabhu teri sharan,
Karo bhakt ka beda paar I
Tere maathe mukut viraj raheo I

ll Aarti Jugal Kishor Ki Kijai ll

Aarti Jugal Kishor Ki Kijai,
Radhe dhan nyouchhavar kijai.
Ravi shashi koti badan ki shobha,
Taahi nirakhi mera man lobha.
Aarti jugal kishor ki kijai... l
Gaur shyam mukh nirakhat reejhai,
Prabhu ko swaroop nayan bhar peejai l
Kanchan thaar kapoor ki baati,
Hari aaye nirmal bhai chhaati l
Aarti jugal kishor ki kijai... l
Phoolan ki sej phoolan ki mala,
Ratan singhasan baithe Nandlala l
Mor mukut kar murli sohai,
Natvar vesh dekhi man mohai l
Aarti jugal kishor ki kijai... l
Aadha neel peet patasari,
Kunj bihari girivardhari l
Shri Purushottam girivardhari,
Aarti karein sakal brajnari l
Aarti jugal kishor ki kijai... l
Nand lala vrishbhanukishori,
Parmanand swami avichal jori l
Aarti jugal kishor ki kijai,
Radhe dhan nyouchhavar kijai l

II Nand-suvan jasumatike lala II

Nand-suvan jasumatike lala,
Godhan gopi priya Gopala I
Devpriya asuran ke kaala,
Mohan vishvavimohan var ki II
Aarti kijai Shrinatvar ji ki I
Govardhan-dhar banshidhar ki II

Jai Vasudev-devaki-nandan,
Kalayavan-kansadi-nikandan I
Jagadadhar ajay jagvandan,
Nitya naveen param sundar ki II
Aarti kijai Shrinatvar ji ki I
Govardhan-dhar banshidhar ki II

Akal kaladhar sakal vishvadhar,
Vishvambar kamad karunakaar I
Ajar, amar, mayik, mayahaar,
Nirgun chinmay gunmandir ki II
Aarti kijai Shrinatvar ji ki I
Govardhan-dhar banshidhar ki II

Pandav-put parikshit rakshak,
Atulit ahi agh mooshak-bhakshak I
Jagmay jagat nireeh nireekshak,
Brahma paratpar parameshwar ki II
Aarti kijai Shrinatvar ji ki I
Govardhan-dhar banshidhar ki II

Nitya satya golokvihari,
Ajavyakt leelavapudhari I
Leelamay leelavistari,
Madhur manohar Radhavar ki II
Aarti kijai Shrinatvar ji ki I
Govardhan-dhar banshidhar ki II

Aarti kijai Shrinatvar ji ki,
Govardhan-dhar banshidhar ki II
Aarti kijai Shrinatvar ji ki,
Govardhan-dhar banshidhar ki II

Aarti kijai Shrinatvar ji ki I
Govardhan-dhar banshidhar ki II

II Aarti Shrikrishna Kanhaiya ki II

Aarti Shrikrishna Kanhaiya ki
Mathura karagrah avatari,
Gokul Jasuda god vihari I
Nandlal Natvar Giradhari,
Vasudev Haladhar bhaiya ki II

Aarti Shrikrishna Kanhaiya ki I
Mor mukut peetambar chhajai,
Kati kaachhani, kar murli virajai I
Poorn sarak sasi mukh lakh lajai,
Kaam koti chhavi jitvaiya ki II

Aarti Shrikrishna Kanhaiya ki I
Gopijan ras raas vilasi,
Kaurav Kaliya, Kans binasi I
Himkar Bhanu, Krisanu prakasi,
Sarvabhoot hiya basvaiya ki II

Aarti Shrikrishna Kanhaiya ki I
Kahu ran chadhai bhagi kahu jaavai,
Kahu nrip kar, kahu gaay charaavai I
Kahu jaages, ved jas gaavai,
Jag nachaay Braj nachvaiya ki II

Aarti Shrikrishna Kanhaiya ki I
Agun sagun leela bapoo dhari,
Anupam Geeta gyaan prachaari I
Damodar sab vidhi balihaari,
Vipra dhenu sur rakhvaiya ki II

II Jai Jai Giridhari II

Jai Jai Giridhari Prabhu, Jai Jai Giridhari I

Daanav-dal-balahari, Go-dwij-hitkari II

Jai Jai Giridhari Prabhu, Jai Jai Giridhari I

Jai Govind Dayanidhi, Govardhan-dhari I

Vanshidhar Banwari, Braj-jan-priykari II

Jai Jai Giridhari Prabhu, Jai Jai Giridhari I

Ganika-geedh-Ajamil-Gajapati-bhayahari I

Aarat-aarati-haari, Jag-mangal-kaari II

Jai Jai Giridhari Prabhu, Jai Jai Giridhari I

Gopalak, Gopeshwar, Draupadi-Dukhdari I

Shabar-suta-sukhkari, Gautam-Tiya tari II

Jai Jai Giridhari Prabhu, Jai Jai Giridhari I

Jan-Prahlad-pramodak, Narhari-tanu-dhari I

Jan-man-ranjankari, Diti-sut-sanhari II

Jai Jai Giridhari Prabhu, Jai Jai Giridhari I

Tittibh-sut-Sanrakshkarakshak Manjhari I

Pandhu-suvan-shubhkarikaurav-mad-hari II

Jai Jai Giridhari Prabhu, Jai Jai Giridhari I

Manmath Manmath Mohan, Murli-rav-kari I

Vrindavipin-vihari, Yamuna-tat-chari II

Jai Jai Giridhari Prabhu, Jai Jai Giridhari I

Agh-bak-baki-udharak Trinavart-tari I

Vidhi-surpati-madhari, Kans-muktikari II

Jai Jai Giridhari Prabhu, Jai Jai Giridhari I

Shesh, Mahesh, Saraswati-gun gavat hari I

Kal kirti-bistari, Bhakt-bhiti-hari II

Jai Jai Giridhari Prabhu, Jai Jai Giridhari I

Narayan Sharanagat, Ati agh, aghahari I

Pad-raj pavankari, Chahat chitahari II

Jai Jai Giridhari Prabhu, Jai Jai Giridhari I

II Shri Yashodalal Aarti II

Aarti karat Yasoda pramudit,
phooli ang na maat I
Bal-bal kahi dularavat,
aanand magan bhai pulkaat II

Subaran-thaar ratna-deepavali
chitrait ghrit-bhini baat I
Kal sindoor doob dadhi achhat,
tilak karat bahu bhaant II

Ann chaturvid bibidhbhog
dundubhi baajat bahu jaat I
Naachat gop kumkumachhirkat
det akhil nagadaat II

Barsat kusum nikar-sur-nar-muni
vrajjuvati muskaat I
Krishnadas-prabhu Giridhar komukh
nirakh lajat sasi-kaant II

॥ Shri Ramchandra Kripalu Bhaju Man ॥

Shri Ramchandra Kripalu Bhaju Man
Haran bhavbhay daarunam ।
Nav kanj lochan,
Kanj mukh kar kanj pad kanjarunam ॥
Shri Ramchandra Kripalu Bhaju Man... ॥

Kandarpa aganit amit chhavi,
Nav neel neerad sundaram ।
Pat peet maanahu tadit
Ruchi-shuchinau mi janak sutavaram ॥
Shri Ramchandra Kripalu Bhaju Man... ॥

Bhaju deenbandhu dineshdaanav
Daitya vansh nikandanam ।
Raghunand aanand kand
Kaushalchandra Dashrath nandnam ॥
Shri Ramchandra Kripalu Bhaju Man... ॥

Sir mukut kundal tilak charu
Udaaru ang vibhushanam ।

Ajaanubhuj shar chaap-dhar,
Sangraam jit khardushanam II

Shri Ramchandra Kripalu Bhaju Man... II

Iti vadati Tulsidas,
Shankar Shesh muni man ranjanam I
Mamah hriday kanj nivaas kuru,
Kaamadi khal dal ganjanam II

Shri Ramchandra Kripalu Bhaju Man... II

Man jahi ra cheu milahiso
Var sahaj sundar saanvaro I
Karuna nidhaan sujaansheel
Saneh jaanat raavaro II

Shri Ramchandra Kripalu Bhaju Man... II

Ehi bhaanti Gauri asis sun
Siy hit hiya harshit ali I
Tulsi bhavani hi puji
Puni-punimudit man mandir chali II

Shri Ramchandra Kripalu Bhaju Man... II

II Aarti Kijai Shri Raghuvar Ji Ki II

Aarti Kijai Shri Raghuvar Ji Ki,
Sat Chit Anand Shiv Sundar Ki I
Dashrath Tanay Kaushalya Nandan,
Sur Muni Rakshak Daitya Nikandan I
Anugat Bhakt Bhakt Ura Chandan,
Maryada Purushottam Var Ki I
Aarti Kijai Shri Raghuvar Ji Ki... I
Nirgun Sagun Anup Roop Nidhi,
Sakal Lok Vandit Vibhinn Vidhi I
Haran Shok-Bhay Dayak Nav Nidhi,
Maya Rahit Divya Nar Var Ki I
Aarti Kijai Shri Raghuvar Ji Ki... I
Janaki Pati Sur Adhipati Jagpati,
Akhil Lok Palak Trilok Gati I
Vishva Vandya Avanh Amit Gati,
Ek Matra Gati Sacharachar Ki I
Aarti Kijai Shri Raghuvar Ji Ki... I
Sharannagat Vatsal Vratdhari,
Bhakt Kalp Taruvar Asurari I
Naam Let Jag Pavnkari,
Vanar Sakha Deen Dukh Har Ki I
Aarti Kijai Shri Raghuvar Ji Ki... I

II Aisi Aarti Ram Raghubeer Ki Karahi Man II

Aisi Aarti Ram Raghubeer Ki Karahi Man
Haran Dukhdund Govind Anandghan II
Aisi Aarti Ram Raghubeer Ki Karahi Man II

Achar Char Roop Hari, Sarvagat,
Sarvada Basat, Iti Basna Dhoop Deeje I
Deep Nijbodhgat Koh-Mad-Moh-Tam
Praudh Abhiman Chittvrutti Chhije II
Aisi Aarti Ram Raghubeer Ki Karahi Man II

Bhav Atishay Vishad Pavar Naivedya Shubh
Shreeraman Param Santoshkari I
Prem-Tambul Gat Shool Sanshay Sakal,
Vipul Bhav-Baasna-Beejhari II
Aisi Aarti Ram Raghubeer Ki Karahi Man II

Ashubh-Shubh Karm Ghritpoorn Dashavartika,
Tyag Pavak, Satogun Prakasam I
Bhakti-Vairagya-Vigyan Deepawali,
Arpi Neerajanam Jaganivasam II
Aisi Aarti Ram Raghubeer Ki Karahi Man II

Bimal Hridi-Bhavan Krit Shanti-Paryank Shubh,
Shayan Vishram Shreeramaraya I
Kshama-Karuna Pramukh Tatra Paricharika,
Yatra Hari Tatra Nahin Bhed-Maya II

Aisi Aarti Ram Raghubeer Ki Karahi Man II

Aarti-Nirat Sanakadi, Shruti, Shesh, Shiv,
Devarishi, Akhilmuni Tattvadarshi I
Karai Soi Tarai, Pariharai Kamadi Mal,
Vadati Iti Amalmati Das Tulsi II

Aisi Aarti Ram Raghubeer Ki Karahi Man II

II Jai Janakinatha II

Jai Janakinatha, Jai Shriraghunatha I
Dou kar joren binvaun, Prabhu! Suniye bata I
Jai Janakinatha, Jai Shriraghunatha I
Tum Raghunath hamare, praan, pita mata I
Tum hi sajjan-sangi, bhakti mukti data I
Jai Janakinatha, Jai Shriraghunatha I
Lakh chaurasi kato meto yam trasa I
Nisidin Prabhu mohi rakhiye apne hi pasa I
Jai Janakinatha, Jai Shriraghunatha I
Ram Bharat Lachhiman sang, shatrun han bhaiya I
Jagmag jyoti virajai, shobha ati lahiya I
Jai Janakinatha, Jai Shriraghunatha I
Hanumat nad bajavat, never jhamkata I
Swarnathal kar aartik Kaushalya mata I
Jai Janakinatha, Jai Shriraghunatha I
Subhag mukut sir, dhanu sarakar sobha bhari I
Maniram darshan kari pal-pal balihari I
Jai Janakinatha, Jai Shriraghunatha I
Jai Janakinatha, Jai Shriraghunatha I
Dou kar joren binvaun, Prabhu! Suniye bata I
Jai Janakinatha, Jai Shriraghunatha I

ll Bandau Raghupati Karuna Nidhan ll

Bandau Raghupati Karuna Nidhan l
Jaate chhootai bhav-bhed gyaan ll
Raghubans-Kumud-Sukhprad Nises l
Sevat pad-pankaj aj-mahes ll
Nij bhakt-hriday pathoj-bhring l
Lavanyabapush aganit anang ll
Ati prabal moh-tam-maratand l
Agyaan-gahan-pavak-prachand ll
Abhiman-sindhu-kumbhaj udar l
Suraranjan, bhanjan bhumibhar ll
Ragadi-sarpagan pannagari l
Kandarpa-nag-mrigpati, Murari ll
Bhav-jaladhi-pot charan-arabind l
Janaki-Ravan anand kand ll
Hanumant prem bapi maral l
Nishkaam kamdhuk go dayal ll
Trailok-tilak, gun-gahan Ram l
Kah Tulsidas vishram-dham ll

ll Aarti Kijai Hanuman Lala Ki ll

Aarti Kijai Hanuman Lala Ki l
Dusht dalan Raghunath kala ki ll
Jake bal se Girivar kape l
Rog dosh jake nikat na jhanke ll

Anjani putra maha baldaai l
Santan ke prabhu sada sahai ll
De beera Raghunath pathaaye l
Lanka jaari Siya sudh laaye ll

Lanka so kot samudra-si khai l
Jaat Pavansut baar na laai ll
Lanka jaari asur sanhaare l
Siyaramji ke kaaj sawaare ll

Lakshman moorchhit pade sakaare l
Aani sanjivan praan ubaare ll
Paithi Pataal tori jam-kaare l
Ahiravan ki bhuja ukhaare ll

Baaye bhuja asurdal maare I
Dahine bhuja santajan taare II
Sur nar muni aarti utaare I
Jai jai jai Hanuman uchaare II

Kanchan thaar kapoor lau chhaai I
Aarti karat Anjana maai II
Jo Hanumanji ki aarti gaave I
Basi Vaikunth param pad paave II

II Ambe tu hai Jagdambe Kal II

Ambe tu hai Jagdambe Kali,
Jai Durge Khappar Wali,
Tere hi gun gaaven Bharti,
O Maiya hum sab utaare Teri Aarti.
O Maiya hum sab utaare Teri Aarti II
Tere bhakt jano par mata
bheer padi hai bhaari I
Danav dal par toot pado
Mankar ke Singh sawari II
Sau-sau sihon se balshaali,
hai Asht bhujaon wali,
Dushton ko tu hi lalkaarti I
O Maiya hum sab utaare Teri Aarti II
Maa-bete ka hai is jag mein
Bada hi nirmal naata I
Poot-kapoot sune hai
Par na mata suni kumata II
Sab pe karuna darshane wali,
Amrit barsane wali,

Dukhiyon ke dukhde nivaarati I

O Maiya hum sab utaare Teri Aarti II

Nahi maangte dhan aur daulat,
Na chaandi na sona I

Hum to maange tere charnon mein
Chhota sa kona II

Sabki bigdi banane wali,
Laaj bachane wali,
Satiyon ke sat ko sanwaarti I

O Maiya hum sab utaare Teri Aarti II

Charan sharan mein khade tumhari,
Le pooja ki thaali I

Varad hast sar par rakh do Maa
Sankat harne wali II

Maa bhar do bhakti ras pyali,
Asht bhujaon wali,
Bhakton ke kaaraj tu hi saarti I

O Maiya hum sab utaare Teri Aarti II

II Mangala ki seva, sun meri deva II

Mangala ki seva, sun meri deva
Haath jod, tere dwar khade I
Paan supari, dhwaja, nariyal,
Le jwala teri bhent dhare II

Mangala ki seva sun meri deva I
Sun Jagdambe, kar na vilambe I
Santan ke bhandar bhare I
Santan-pratipali, sada khushhaali,
Maiya jai Kali kalyaan kare II

Mangala ki seva sun meri deva I
Buddhi vidhata, tu jag mata,
Mera kaaraj siddh kare I
Charan kamal ka liya aasra,
Sharan tumhari aan pare II

Mangala ki seva sun meri deva I
Jab-jab bhir padi bhaktan par,
Tab-tab aay sahaay kare I
Baar-baar tain sab jag mohayo,
Taruni roop anoop dhare II

Mangala ki seva sun meri deva I
Mata hokar putr khilave,

Kahin bharya bhog kare I
Santan sukhdaayi sada sahayi,
Santan khade jaykaar kare II
Mangala ki seva sun meri deva I
Brahma Vishnu Mahesh sahasaphan liye,
Bhent den tere dwar khade I
Atal sihaansan baithi meri mata,
Sir sone ka chhatra phire II
Mangala ki seva sun meri deva I
Vaar Shanichar kunkum barano,
Jab lunkad par hukam kare I
Khadg khappar trishul haath liye,
Rakt beej ko bhasm kare II
Mangala ki seva sun meri deva I
Shumbh Nishumbh ko kshan mein mare,
Mahishasur ko pakad dale I
'Aadit' vaari aadi bhavani,
Jan apne ka kasht hare II
Mangala ki seva sun meri deva I
Kupit hoy danav mare,
Chand mund sab choor kare I
Jab tum dekhi daya roop ho,

Pal mein sankat door kare II

Mangala ki seva sun meri deva I

Saumya swabhav dharyo meri mata,
Jan ki arj kabool kare I
Saat baar ki mahima barni,
Sab gun kaun bakhan kare II

Mangala ki seva sun meri deva I

Singh peeth par chadhi bhavani,
Atal bhavan mein raaj kare I
Darshan paaven mangal gaaven,
Siddh saadhak teri bhent dhare II

Mangala ki seva sun meri deva I

Brahma ved padhe tere dware,
Shiv shankar dhyan dhare I
Indra Krishna teri kare aarti,
Chanwar Kuber dulay rahe II

Mangala ki seva sun meri deva I

Jai janani jai matu bhavani,
Atal bhavan mein raaj kare I
Santan pratipali sada khushhaali,
Maiya jai Kali kalyaan kare II

Mangala ki seva sun meri deva II

II Aarti Durga ji ki kijiye II

Aarti Durga ji ki kijiye,
Dukh daridra vinaashini sejiye II

Jo jan nit gaave man laayi,
Ta par maan prasann ho jaayi II

Durga roop niraala Bhavani,
Shiv sang subhag shobha vakhaani II

Kar mein khadg trishool viraaje,
Dusht dalan kar kaal samaaje II

Rakt Chandi maatu varadaayini,
Bhakt janon ki man sukhadaayini II

Singh vaahini jai jai mataa,
Tribhuvan mein tu shakti daataa II

Jai Ambe Gauri jai Shivraani,
Tere charano ki vandan vaanee II

II Jai Ambe Gauri Aarti II

Jai Ambe Gauri, Maiya Jai Shyama Gauri I
Tumko nishidin dhyavat, Hari Brahma
Shivari II Om Jai Ambe Gauri II

Maang sindoor virajat, teeko mrigmad ko I
Ujjval se dou naina, chandravadana neeko
IIOm Jai Ambe Gauri II

Kanak saman kalevar, raktambar raaje I
Raktpushp galmala, kanthan par saaje II
Om Jai Ambe Gauri II
Kehri vahan raajat, khadg khappardhaari I
Sur-nar-muni jan sevat, tinke dukhhaari II
Om Jai Ambe Gauri II

Kanan kundal shobhit, nasagre moti I
Kotik chandra divakar, sam raajat jyoti II
Om Jai Ambe Gauri II

Shumbh-nishumbh bidaare, Mahishasur ghaati I
Dhoomravilochan naina, nishidin madmaati
Om Jai Ambe Gauri II
Chand-mund sanhaare, shonit beej hare I

Madhukaitabh dou haare, sur bhayheen kare II Om Jai Ambe Gauri II

Brahmani, Rudrani, tum Kamala raani I
Aagam-nigam-bakhani, tum Shiv patraani II
Om Jai Ambe Gauri II

Chausath yogini gaavat, nritya karat Bhairu
Bajat taal mridanga, aru bajat damaru II
Om Jai Ambe Gauri II
Tum hi jag ki mata, tum hi ho bharta I
Bhaktan ki dukh harta, sukh sampatti karta
Om Jai Ambe Gauri II

Bhuja chaar ati shobhit, var mudra dhaari I
Manvanchhit phal paavat, sevat nar-naari II
Om Jai Ambe Gauri II
Kanchan thaal virajat, agar kapoor baati I
Shri Malketu mein raajat, koti ratan jyoti II
Om Jai Ambe Gauri II

Ambe ji ki aarti, jo koi nar gaave I
Kahat Shivanand Swami, sukh-sampatti paave II Om Jai Ambe Gauri II

II Aarti Mata Bhavani Ki II

Aarti Mata Bhavani Ki,
Maa Jagdamba Bhavani Ki II

Lal chunariya odhe
tu sher pe sawaari,
Tera roop hai sundar,
tu jag se nyaari II

Mathe pe bindiya chamke,
haathon mein talwar,
Dushton ka naash kare,
kare bhakton ka uddhaar II

Tere naam ka pyala,
jo koi piye maa,
Bhavsagar se tar jaye,
dukh door ho maa II

Aarti Mata Bhavani Ki,
Maa Ambe Bhavani Ki II

II Durge durghat bhaari II

Durge durghat bhaari tujvin sansaari –
Anaathnaathe Ambe karuna vistari II
Vaari vaari janma maranante vaari –
Haari padlo aata sankat nivaari II 1 II

Jai Devi jai Devi Mahishasurmathini –
Suravar Ishwar varade tarak sanjeevani
Jai Devi jai Devi II Dhru II

Tribhuvan bhuvani paahata tuj aisi naahi
Chaari shramle parantu na bolave kahi
Saahi vivaad karita padle pravahi –
Te tu bhaktanna paavsi lav laahi II 2 II

Prasanna vadane prasanna hosi nijdasa
Kleshaanpasun todi todvi bhavpasha –
Ambe tujvachun kon purvil asha –
Narhar tallin jhala padpankajlesha II

II Jai Vaishnavi Mata II

Jai Vaishnavi Mata, Maiya Jai Vaishnavi Mata I
Haath jod tere aage, Aarti main gaata II
Sheesh pe chhatra viraje, moortiya pyaari I
Ganga bahti charanan, jyoti jage nyaari II

Brahma ved padhe nit dware,
Shankar dhyan dhare I
Sevak chanwar dulavat, Narad nritya kare II
Sundar gufa tumhari, man ko ati bhaave I
Baar-baar dekhan ko, ai maa man chaave II

Bhavan pe jhande jhoolein,
ghanta dhvani baaje I
Uncha parvat tera, mata priya laage II
Paan supari dhwaja nariyal, bhent pushp mewa I
Das khade charanon mein,darshan dodeva II

Jo jan nishchay karke, dwaar tere aave I
Uski ichha poorn, mata ho jaave II
Itni stuti nish-din, jo nar bhi gaave I
Kahte sevak dhyanu, sukh sampatti paave II

II Navdurga Ki Aarti II

II Aarti Devi Shailputri Ji Ki II

Shailputri Maa bail aswaar I
Karein devta jai jai kaar II
Shiv-Shankar ki priya Bhavani I
Teri mahima kisi ne na jaani II
Parvati tu Uma kehlaave I
Jo tujhe sumire so sukh paave II
Riddhi Siddhi parwan karein tu I
Daya karein dhanwan karein tu II
Somvar ko Shiv sang pyaari I
Aarti jisne teri utaari II
Uski sagri aas puja do I
Sagare dukh takleef mita do II
Ghee ka sundar deep jala ke I
Gola gari ka bhog laga ke II
Shraddha bhaav se mantra japayein I
Prem sahit phir sheesh jhukayein II
Jai Giriraj Kishori Ambe I
Shiv mukh chandra chakori Ambe II
Manokamna poorn kar do I
Chaman sada sukh sampatti bhar do II

II Aarti Devi Brahmacharini Ji Ki II

Jai Ambe Brahmacharini Mata I
Jai Chaturanan Priya Sukh Data II
Brahma Ji ke man bhaati ho I
Gyaan sabhi ko sikhlaati ho II
Brahm mantra hai jaap tumhaara I
Jisko jape saral sansaara II
Jai Gayatri Ved ki Mata I
Jo jan jis din tumhe dhyaata II
Kami koi rahne na paaye I
Koi bhi dukh sahne na paaye II
Uski virati rahe thikaane I
Jo teri mahima ko jaane II
Rudraksha ki mala le kar I
Jape jo mantra shraddha de kar II
Aalas chhod kare gun gaana I
Maa tum usko sukh pahunchana II
Brahmacharini tero naam I
Poorn karo sab mere kaam II
Bhakt tere charanon ka pujari I
Rakhna laaj meri mahatari II

II Aarti Devi Chandraghanta Ji Ki II

Jai Maa Chandraghanta Sukh Dhaam I
Poorn Keejo Mere Kaam II
Chandra Samaaj Tu Sheetal Daati I
Chandra Tej Kiranon Mein Samaati II
Man Ki Maalak Man Bhaati Ho I
Chandraghanta Tum Var Daati Ho II
Sundar Bhaav Ko Laane Wali I
Har Sankat Mein Bachane Wali II
Har Budhwaar Ko Tujhe Dhyaaye I
Shraddha Sahit To Vinay Sunaaye II
Moorti Chandra Aakaar Banaaye I
Sanmukh Ghee Ki Jyot Jalaaye II
Sheesh Jhuka Kahe Man Ki Baata I
Poorn Aas Karo Jagat Daata II
Kaanchipur Sthaan Tumhaara I
Karnatika Mein Maan Tumhaara II
Naam Tera Ratu Maharani I
Bhakt Ki Raksha Karo Bhavaani II

II Aarti Devi Kushmanda Ji Ki II

Kushmanda Jai Jag Sukhdaani I
Mujh Par Daya Karo Maharaani II
Pingala Jwalamukhi Niraali I
Shaakambari Maa Bholi Bhaali II
Laakhon Naam Niraale Tere I
Bhakt Kai Matwaale Tere II
Bheema Parvat Par Hai Dera I
Sveekaaro Pranaam Ye Mera II
Sabki Sunti Ho Jagdambe I
Sukh Pahunchaati Ho Maa Ambe II
Tere Darshan Ka Main Pyaasa I
Poorn Kar Do Meri Aasha II
Maa Ke Mann Mein Mamta Bhaari I
Kyon Na Sunegi Arj Hamaari II
Tere Dar Par Kiya Hai Dera I
Door Karo Maa Sankat Mera II
Mere Kaaj Poore Kar Do I
Mere Tum Bhandare Bhar Do II
Tera Daas Tujhe Hi Dhyaaye I
Bhakt Tere Dar Sheesh Jhukaaye II

ll Aarti Devi Skandamata Ji Ki ll

Jai Teri Ho Skand Mata l
Paanchva Naam Tumhaara Aata ll
Sabke Man Ki Jaanan Haari l
Jag Janani Sabki Mahataari ll
Teri Jyot Jalaata Rahoon Main l
Hardam Tujhe Dhyaata Rahoon Mai ll
Kai Naamon Se Tujhe Pukaara l
Mujhe Ek Hai Tera Sahaara ll
Kahi Pahaadon Par Hai Dera l
Kai Shehron Mein Tera Basera ll
Har Mandir Mein Tere Nazaare l
Gun Gaaye Tere Bhakt Pyaare ll
Bhakti Apni Mujhe Dila Do l
Shakti Meri Bigdi Bana Do ll
Indra Aadi Devta Mil Saare l
Kare Pukaar Tumhaare Dwaare ll
Dusht Daitya Jab Chad Kar Aaye l
Tu Hi Khand Haath Uthaaye ll
Dason Ko Sada Bachane Aayi l
Bhakt Ki Aas Pujane Aayi ll

II Aarti Devi Katyayani Ji Ki II

Jai Jai Ambe Jai Katyayani I
Jai Jag Mata Jag Ki Maharani II
Baijnath Sthan Tumhaara I
Vahavar Daati Naam Pukaara II
Kai Naam Hai Kai Dhaam Hai I
Yah Sthan Bhi To Sukh Dhaam Hai II
Har Mandir Mein Jyot Tumhaari I
Kahi Yogeshwari Mahima Nyaari II
Har Jagah Utsav Hote Rahte I
Har Mandir Mein Bhagat Hai Kehte II
Katyayani Rakshak Kaaya Ki I
Granthi Kaate Moh Maya Ki II
Jhoothe Moh Se Chhudaane Waali I
Apna Naam Japaane Waali II
Brihaspativaar Ko Pooja Kariye I
Dhyaan Katyayani Ka Dhariye II
Har Sankat Ko Door Karegi I
Bhandare Bharpoor Karegi II
Jo Bhi Maa Ko Bhakt Pukaare I
Katyayani Sab Kasht Nivaare II

ll Aarti Devi Kalaratri Ji Ki ll

Kalaratri Jai Jai Mahakaali l
Kaal ke munh se bachaane waali ll
Dusht sanghaarakk naam tumhaara l
Mahachandi tera avataara ll
Prithvi aur aakaash pe saara l
Mahakaali hai tera pasaara ll
Khadg khappar rakhne waali l
Dushton ka lahoo chakhne waali ll
Kalkatta sthan tumhaara l
Sab jagah dekhun tera najara ll
Sabhi devta sab nar-naari l
Gaaven stuti sabhi tumhaari ll
Raktadantaa aur Annapoorna l
Kripa kare to koi bhi dukh naa ll
Naa koi chinta rahe naa beemaari l
Naa koi gham naa sankat bhaari ll
Us par kabhi kasht naa aave l
Mahakaali maa jise bachaave ll
Tu bhi bhakt prem se kah l
Kalaratri maa teri jai ll

II Aarti Devi Mahagauri Ji Ki II

Jai Mahagauri jagat ki maya I
Jai Uma Bhavani jai Mahamaya II
Haridwar Kanakhal ke pasa I
Mahagauri tera waha nivaas II
Chandrakali aur mamta Ambe I
Jai Shakti jai jai maa Jagdambe II
Bhima Devi Vimala mata I
Kaushik Devi jag vikhyata II
Himachal ke ghar Gauri roop tera I
Mahakali Durga hai swaroop tera II
Sati (Sat) havan kund mein tha jalaya I
Usi dhuen ne roop Kaali banaya II
Bana dharm singh jo sawaari mein aaya I
To Shankar ne trishool apna dikhaya II
Tabhi maa ne Mahagauri naam paaya I
Sharan aanewale ka sankat mitaya II
Shanivaar ko teri pooja jo karta I
Maa bigda hua kaam uska sudharta II
Bhakt bolo to soch tum kya rahe ho I
Mahagauri maa teri hardam hi jai ho II

II Aarti Devi Siddhidatri Ji Ki II

Jai Siddhidatri maa tu siddhi ki data I
Tu bhakton ki rakshak tu dason ki mata II
Tera naam lete hi milti hai siddhi I
Tere naam se man ki hoti hai shuddhi II
Kathin kaam siddh karti ho tum I
Tabhi haath sevak ke sir dharti ho tum II
Teri pooja mein to na koi vidhi hai I
Tu Jagdambe dati tu sarv siddhi hai II
Ravivaar ko tera sumiran kare jo I
Teri murti ko hi man mein dhare jo II
Tu sab kaaj uske karti hai poore I
Kabhi kaam uske rahe na adhoore II
Tumhari daya aur tumhari yeh maya I
Rakhe jiske sir par Maiya apni chhaya II
Sarv siddhi dati vah hai bhagyashaali I
Jo hai tere dar ka hi ambe sawali II
Himachal hai parvat jahan vaas tera I
Mahananda mandir mein hai vaas tera II
Mujhe aasra hai tumhara hi mata I
Bhakti hai sawali tu jiski data II

II Shri Parvati Mata Ki Aarti II

Jai Parvati Mata Jai Parvati Mata I
Brahma Sanatan Devi
Shubh Phal Ki Data II

Jai Parvati Mata
Arikul Padma Vinashin
Jai Sevak Trata I

Jag Jeevan Jagdamba,
Harihar Gun Gata II

Jai Parvati Mata
Singh Ko Vahan Saaje,
Kundal Hain Saatha I

Dev Vadhu Jas Gavat,
Nritya Karat Tatha II

Jai Parvati Mata
Satyug Roopshil Atisundar,
Naam Sati Kehlata I

Hemanchal Ghar Janmi,
Sakhiyaan Sang Raata II

Jai Parvati Mata
Shumbh Nishumbh Vidare,

Hemanchal Sthata I

Sahasra Bhuja Tanu Dhari Ke,
Chakra Liyo Haatha II

Jai Parvati Mata
Srishti Roop Tuhi Hai Janani,
Shiva Sang Rangrata I
Nandi Bhrringi Been Lahi
Sara Jag Madmata II

Jai Parvati Mata
Devan Arj Karata Ham
Chit Ko Lata I
Gavat De De Taali,
Man Mein Rangrata II

Jai Parvati Mata
Shri Pratap Aarti Maiya Ki,
Jo Koi Gata I
Sada Sukhi Nit Rahata
Sukha Sampatti Pata II

Jai Parvati Mata

II Shri Bagalamukhi Mata Ji Ki Aarti II

Jai jai Shri Bagalamukhi Mata,
Aarti karahu tumhari. (x2)
Peet vasan tan par tav sohai,
Kundal ki chhabi nyari II

Kar-kamlon mein mudgar dharai,
Astuti karahin sakal nar-nari II

Jai jai Shri Bagalamukhi Mata...
Champak maal gale lahrave,
Sur nar muni jai jai ti uchari II

Trividha taap miti jat sakal sab,
Bhakti sada tav hai sukhkari II

Jai jai Shri Bagalamukhi Mata...
Paalat harat srijat tum jag ko,
Sab jeevan ki ho rakhwari II

Moh nisha mein bhramat sakal jan,
Karahu hriday me tum ujiari II

Jai jai Shri Bagalamukhi Mata...
Timir nashavahu gyan badhavahu,

Ambe tumhi ho asurari II
Santan ko sukh det sada hi,
Sab jan ki tum pran piyari II

Jai jai Shri Bagalamukhi Mata...
Tav charanan jo dhyan lagavai,
Tako ho sab bhav-bhaya hari II
Prem sahit jo karahin aarti,
Te nar mokshdham adhikari II

Jai jai Shri Bagalamukhi Mata...

Doha:
Bagalamukhi ki aarti, padhe sunhe jo koy I
Vinti bhagat ki, sukh-sampati sab hoy I

II Shri Vindhyeshwari Mata Ji Ki Aarti II

Sun meri devi parvatvasini,
Tera paar na paya. (x2)
Paan supari dhwaja nariyal,
Le teri bhent chadhaya II
Jai Vindhyeshwari Mata II

Suwa choli tere ang virajai,
Keshar tilak lagaya I
Nange paon Akbar jakar,
Sone ka chhatra chadhaya II
Jai Vindhyeshwari Mata II

Unche unche parvat bana devalay,
Neeche shahar basaya I
Satyug Treta Dwapar madhye,
Kalyug raj savaya II
Jai Vindhyeshwari Mata II

Dhoop deep naivedya aarti,
Mohan bhog lagaya I
Dhyanu bhagat Maiya (tera) gun gawai,
Man vanchhit phal paya II
Jai Vindhyeshwari Mata II

II Aarti Lalita Mata Ki II

Shri Mateshwari Jai Tripureshwari I
Rajeshwari Jai Namo Namah II
Karunamayi Sakal Agh Harini I
Amrit Varshini Namo Namah II
Jai Sharanam Varanam Namo Namah I
Shri Mateshwari Jai Tripureshwari II
Ashubh Vinashini, Sab Sukh Dayini I
Khal-Dal Nashini Namo Namah II
Bhandasur Vadhkarini Jai Maa I
Karuna Kalite Namo Namah II
Jai Sharanam Varanam Namo Namah I
Shri Mateshwari Jai Tripureshwari II
Bhav Bhay Harini, Kasht Nivarini I
Sharan Gati Do Namo Namah II
Shiv Bhamini Sadhak Man Harini I
Adi Shakti Jai Namo Namah II
Jai Sharanam Varanam Namo Namah I
Jai Tripur Sundari Namo Namah II
Shri Mateshwari Jai Tripureshwari I
Rajeshwari Jai Namo Namah II

II Om Mahalaxmyai Namo Namah II

Namaste tu Mahamaye
Shri Peethe Surapoojite
Shankh Chakra Gada Haste
Mahalaxmi Namostute, Namostute
Om Mahalaxmyai Namo Namah
Om Vishnupriyayai Namo Namah
Om Dhanapradayai Namo Namah
Om Vishwajannyai Namo Namah
Om Mahalaxmyai Namo Namah
Om Vishnupriyayai Namo Namah
Om Dhanapradayai Namo Namah
Om Vishwajannyai Namo Namah
Om Mahalaxmyai Namo Namah
Om Vishnupriyayai Namo Namah
Om Dhanapradayai Namo Namah
Om Vishwajannyai Namo Namah
Om Mahalaxmyai Namo Namah
Om Vishnupriyayai Namo Namah
Om Dhanapradayai Namo Namah
Om Vishwajannyai Namo Namah

II Om Jai Lakshmi Mata II

Om Jai Lakshmi Mata,
Maiya Jai Lakshmi Mata.
Tumko Nishdin Sevat,
Har Vishnu Vidhata. || Om Jai… ||
Uma, Rama se Milkar,
Tum Bhav Nidhi Pata.
Jo Koi Tumko Dhyata,
Riddhi-Siddhi Pata. || Om Jai… ||
Tum Patal Nivasini,
Tum Hi Shubhadaata.
Karma-Prabhav-Prakashini,
Bhav Nidhi Ki Traata. || Om Jai… ||
Jis Ghar Mein Tum Rehti,
Sab Sadgun Aata.
Sab Sambhav Ho Jata,
Man Nahin Ghabrata. || Om Jai… ||
Tum Bin Yagya Na Hote,
Vastra Na Koi Pata.
Khan-Paan Ka Vaibhav,
Sab Tumse Aata. || Om Jai… ||
Shubhgun Mandir Sundar,
Ksheerodadhi Jata.
Ratna Chaturdash Saath Lai,
Sab Man Ko Bhata. || Om Jai… ||
Mahalakshmi Ji Ki Aarti, Jo Koi Jan Gata.
Ura Anand Samata, Paap Utar Jata. ||
Om Jai Lakshmi Mata, Maiya Jai
Lakshmi Mata.

II Shri Annapurna Mata ji ki Aarti II

Shri Annapurna Mata ji ki Aarti
Barambar pranam,
Maiya barambar pranam.
Jo nahin dhyave tumhein Ambike,
Kahan use vishram.
Annapurna Devi naam tihare,
Lete hot sab kaam.
Pralay yugantar aur janmantar,
Kalanter tak naam.
Sur suron ki rachna karti,
Kahan Krishna kahan Ram.
Choomahi charan chatur chaturanan,
Charu chakradhar shyam.
Chandra chud chandranan chakar,
Shobha lakhahi lalam.
Devi dev dayaniy dasha mein,
Daya daya tav naam.
Traahi-traahi sharanagat vatsal,
Sharan roop tav dhaam.
Shreem, hreem, shraddha,
shreem aim vidya,
Shreem kleem kamal kaam.
Kantibhraintimayi kanti shantimayi,
Var detu nishkaam.

II Aarti Sri Santoshi Maa ki II

Jai Santoshi Mata,
Maiya Jai Santoshi Mata.
Apne sevak jan ko,
sukh sampatti data.
Jai Santoshi Mata.
Sundar cheer sunahri,
ma dharan kinho.
Heera panna damke,
tan shringar kinho.
Jai Santoshi Mata.
Geru lal chhata chhavi,
badan kamal sohe.
Mand hansat karunamayi,
tribhuvan man mohe.
Jai Santoshi Mata.
Swarn singhasan baithi,
chanvar dhure pyare.
Dhoop deep madhumeva,
bhog dhare nyare.
Jai Santoshi Mata.
Gud aru chana parampriya,
tame santosh kiyo.
Santoshi kehlai, bhaktan vaibhav diyo.
Jai Santoshi Mata.
Shukravar priya manat, aaj divas sohi.

Bhakt mandali chhai,
katha sunat mohi.
Jai Santoshi Mata.
Mandir jagmag jyoti, mangal dhvani
chhai.Vinay karein hum balak,
charnan sir naai
Jai Santoshi Mata
Bhakti bhavamay pooja, angikrit kije
Jo man basai hamare, ichha phal dijiye
Jai Santoshi Mata
Dukhi daridri, rog, sankat mukt kiye
Bahu dhan-dhanya bhare ghar,
sukh saubhagya diye
Jai Santoshi Mata
Dhyan dharyo jis jan ne,
manvanchhit phal payo
Pooja katha shravan kar,
ghar anand aayo
Jai Santoshi Mata
Sharan gahe ki lajja,
rakhiyo Jagdambe
Sankat tu hi nivare, dayamayi Ambe
Jai Santoshi Mata
Santoshi Mata ki aarti, jo koi jan gaave
Riddhi-siddhi, sukh-sampatti,
jee bharkar paave
Jai Santoshi Mata

II Jai Saraswati Mata II

Jai Saraswati Mata,
Maiya Jai Saraswati Mata
Sadgun vaibhav shalini,
tribhuvan vikhyata
Jai Saraswati Mata
Chandravadani padmasini,
dyuti mangalkari
Sohe shubh hans savari, atul tejdhari
Jai Saraswati Mata
Baen kar mein veena, daen kar mala
Sheesh mukut mani sohe,
gal motiyan mala
Jai Saraswati Mata
Devi sharan jo aaye, unka uddhar kiya
Paithi Manthara dasi, Ravan sanhar kiya
Jai Saraswati Mata
Vidya gyan pradayini,
gyan prakaash bharo
Moh agyan aur timir ka, jag se nash karo
Jai Saraswati Mata
Dhoop deep phal mewa, maa svikar karo
Gyanchakshu de mata, jag nistaar karo
Jai Saraswati Mata
Maa Saraswati ki aarti, jo koi jan gaave
Hitkari sukhkari gyan bhakti paave
Jai Saraswati Mata
Sadgun vaibhav shalini,
tribhuvan vikhyata
Jai Saraswati Mata

II Bhuvan viraji Sharada II

Bhuvan viraji Sharada
mahima aparampar
Bhakton ke kalyan ko
dharo maat avatar
Maiya Sharada tore darbar
Aarti nit gaun x3
Nit gaun Maiya
Nit gaun x2
Maiya Sharada tore darbar
Aarti nit gaun x2

Shraddha ko diya preet ki baati
Asuan tel chadhaun x2
Darsh tore paun
Maiya Sharada tore darbar
Aarti nit gaun x3

Man ki mala aankh ke moti
Bhaav ke phool chadhaun x2
Darsh tore paun
Maiya Sharada tore darbar
Aarti nit gaun x3

Bal ko bhog swaans din rati
Kandhe se vinay sunaun x2
Darsh tore paun

II Ya Kundendu-tushara-hara-dhavala II

Ya Kundendu-tushara-hara-dhavala
Ya shubhra-vastravrita
Ya veena-vara-danda-manditakara
Ya shveta-padmasana
Ya Brahma-achyuta Shankara-
prabhritibhir devaih sada vandita
Sa mam patu Sarasvati Bhagavati
nihshesha-jaadya-apaha

Shuklam Brahma-vichara-sara
paramaam adyam jagad-vyapinim
Veena-pustaka-dharinim abhayadam
jaadya-andhakara-apaham
Haste sphatika-malikam vidadhatim
padmasane samsthitam
Vande tam parameshvarim
Bhagavatim buddhipradam Sharadam

II He Hansavahini Gyan Dayini II

He Hansavahini Gyan Dayini
Amb Vimal Mati De
Amb Vimal Mati De
He Hansavahini Gyan Dayini
Amb Vimal Mati De
Amb Vimal Mati De
Jag Siramore Banayen Bharat
Vah Bal Vikram De
Vah Bal Vikram De
He Hansavahini Gyan Dayini
Amb Vimal Mati De
Amb Vimal Mati De
Sahas Sheel Hriday Mein Bhar De
Jeevan Tyag-Tapomay Kar De
Sahas Sheel Hriday Mein Bhar De
Jeevan Tyag-Tapomay Kar De
Sanyam Satya Sneh Ka Var De
Swabhiman Bhar De
Sanyam Satya Sneh Ka Var De
Swabhiman Bhar De I
He Hansavahini Gyan Dayini
Amb Vimal Mati De

Amb Vimal Mati De
Lav-Kush Dhruv Prahlad Banen Hum
Manavta Ka Tras Harein Hum
Lav-Kush Dhruv Prahlad Banen Hum
Manavta Ka Tras Harein Hum
Sita Savitri Durga Maa
Phir Ghar-Ghar Bhar De
Sita Savitri Durga Maa
Phir Ghar-Ghar Bhar De I

He Hansavahini Gyan Dayini
Amb Vimal Mati De
Amb Vimal Mati De
Amb Vimal Mati De

II Jayati Jay Jay Maa Saraswati II

Jayati Jay Jay Maa Saraswati,
Jayati Veena Dharini II

Jayati Padmasana Mata,
Jayati Shubh Varadayini I

Jayati Jay Jay Maa Saraswati,
Jayati Veena Dharini II

Jagat ka Kalyan kar Maa,
Tum ho Veena Vadini I

Jayati Jay Jay Maa Saraswati,
Jayati Veena Dharini II

Kamal Aasan chhodkar aa,
Dekh meri durdasha Maa I

Jayati Jay Jay Maa Saraswati,
Jayati Veena Dharini II

Gyaan ki Sarita baha Maa,
He sakal JagataraNi I

Jayati Jay Jay Maa Saraswati,
Jayati Veena Dharini II

II Om Jai Gange Mata II

Om Jai Gange Mata,
Maiya Jai Gange Mata I
Jo nar tumko dhyata,
manvanchhit phal pata II
Om Jai Gange Mata II
Chandra-si jyoti tumhari,
jal nirmal aata I
Sharan pade jo teri,
so nar tar jata II
Om Jai Gange Mata II
Putra sagar ke tare, sab jag ko gyata I
Kripa drishti ho tumhari,
tribhuvan sukh data II
Om Jai Gange Mata II
Ek bar jo prani, sharan teri aata I
Yam ki tras mitakar, paramgati pata II
Om Jai Gange Mata II
Aarti matu tumhari, jo nar nit gata I
Sevak wahi sahaj me, mukti ko pata II
Om Jai Gange Mata II

II Jai Jai Bhagirathanandini II

Jai jai bhagirathanandini,
muni-chaya chakor-chandini,
nar-nag-bibudh-bandini, jai jahnubaalika I

Jai jai bhagirathanandini... I
Vishnu-pad-sarojjasi,
eesa-sees par bibhaasi,
tripathgasi, punyaraasi, paap-chhaalika II

Jai jai bhagirathanandini... I
Bimal bipul bahasi baari,
seetal trayataap-haari,
bhanvar bar bibhangatartarang-maalika I

Jai jai bhagirathanandini... I
Purajan poojophaar
sobhitasasi dhaval dhaar,
bhanjan bhav-bhaar, bhakti-kalp thaalika II

Jai jai bhagirathanandini... I
Nij tat baasi bihang,
jal-thal-char pasu-patang,
keet, jatil tapas, sab saris paalika I

Jai jai bhagirathanandini... I
Tulsi tava teer teersumirat raghuvans-beer,
bicharat mati dehimoha-mahish-kaalika II

Jai jai bhagirathanandini... I

II Shri Narmada Mata Ji Ki Aarti II

Om Jai Jagadanandi,
Maiya Jai Anand Kandi I
Brahma Harihar Shankar Rewa,
Shiv Hari Shankar Rudri Palanti II

Om Jai Jagadanandi... II
Devi Narad Sharad Tum Varadayak,
Abhinav Padchandi I
Sur Nar Muni Jan Sevat,
Sur Nar Muni Sharad Padvanti II

Om Jai Jagadanandi... II
Devi Dhoomak Vahan Rajat,
Veena Vadayanti I
Jhumkat Jhumkat Jhumkat,
Jhananan Jhananan Ramati Rajanti II

Om Jai Jagadanandi... II
Devi Bajat Taal Mridanga,
Surmandal Ramati II
Tooditaan Tooditaan Tooditaan,
Turadad Turadad Turadad
Ramti Survanti II
Tooreetaan Tooreetaan Tooreetaan,

Turadad Turadad Turadad Ramatee Suravantee II

Om Jai Jagadanandi... II

Devi Sakal Bhuvan Par Aap Virajat,
Nishadin Anandi I

Gavat Ganga Shankar, Sevat Reva
Shankar Tum Bhav Metanti II

Om Jai Jagadanandi... II

Maiyaa Ji Ko Kanchan Thaal Virajat,
Agar Kapoor Baati I

Amarakant Mein Virajat,
Ghatan Ghaat Koti Ratan Jyoti II

Om Jai Jagadanandi... II

Maiyaa Ji Ki Aarti Nishadin Padhi Gaavein,
Ho Reva Jug Jug Nar Gaavein I

Bhajat Shivaanand Swami,
Japat Hari Man Vaanchhit Phal Paavein II

Om Jai Jagadanandi... II

II Yamuna Mata Aarti II

Om Jai Yamuna Mata,
Hari Om Jai Yamuna Mata I
Jo nahave phal paave sukh dukh ki data II
Om Jai Yamuna Mata... II
Pavan Shriyamuna jal sheetal
agam baha dhara I
Jo jan sharan mein aaya kar diya nistara II
Om Jai Yamuna Mata... II
Jo jan pratah hi uthkar nitya snaan kare I
Yam ke traas na paave jo nitya dhyan kare II
Om Jai Yamuna Mata... II
Kalikaal mein mahima tumhari atal rahi I
Tumhara bada mahatam charon ved kahi II
Om Jai Yamuna Mata... II
Aan tumhare mata prabhu avatar liyo I
Nitya nirmal jal peekar kans ko maar diyo II
Om Jai Yamuna Mata... II
Namo mat bhay harani
shubh mangal karni I
Man bechain bhaya hai tum bin vaitarani II
Om Jai Yamuna Mata... II
Om Jai Yamuna Mata,
Hari Om Jai Yamuna Mata I
Jo nahave phal paave sukh dukh ki data II
Om Jai Yamuna Mata... II

II A a r t i Ahoi Mata ki II

Jai Ahoi Mata, Jai Ahoi Mata I
Tumko nisdin dhyavat har Vishnu vidhata II
Jai Ahoi Mata... II
Brahmani, Rudrani kamlatu hi hai jagmata I
Surya-Chandrama dhyavat
Narad rishi gata II
Jai Ahoi Mata... II
Mata roop niranjan sukh-sampatti data I
Jo koi tumko dhyavat nit mangal pata II
Jai Ahoi Mata... II
Tu hi patal basanti, tu hi hai shubhdata I
Karma-prabhav prakashak
jaganidhi se trata II
Jai Ahoi Mata... II
Jis ghar tharo vasawahi mein gun aata I
Kar na sake soi kar le man nahi dhadkata II
Jai Ahoi Mata... II
Tum bin sukh na hoven koi putra pata I
Khan-paan ka vaibhav tum bin nahi aata II
Jai Ahoi Mata... II
Shubh gun sundar yukta akshir nidhi jata I
Ratan chaturdash toku koi nahi pata II
Jai Ahoi Mata... II
Shri Ahoi Maa ki aarti jo koi gata I
Ura umang ati upje paap utar jata II
Jai Ahoi Mata... II

II Ekadashi Mata Ki Aarti II

Om Jai Ekadashi, Jai Ekadashi,
Jai Ekadashi Mata I
Vishnu pooja vrat ko dhaaran kar,
Shakti mukti paata II Om Jai Ekadashi... II
Tere naam ginaoon devi,
bhakti pradaan karni I
Gan gaurav ki deni mata,
shastro mein varni II Om Jai Ekadashi... II
Margashirsha ke krishna paksh ki utpanna,
vishvatarni janmi I
Shukla paksh mein hui mokshada,
muktidata ban aai II Om Jai Ekadashi... II
Paush ke krishna paksh ki, safala naamak
hai I
Shukla paksh mein hoy putrada,
anand adhik rahai II Om Jai Ekadashi... II
Naam Shatatila Maagh Maas Mein,
Krishna Paksh Aavai,
Shukla Paksh Mein Jaya, Kahavai, Vijay
Sada Paavai II Om Jai Ekadashi... II
Vijaya Phagun Krishna Paksh Mein
Shukla Aamalaki,
Paapmochani Krishna Paksh Mein,
Chaitra Mahaabali Ki II Om Jai Ekadashi... II

Chaitra Shukla Mein Naam Kaamada,
Dhan Dene Wali,
Naam Varuthini Krishna Paksh Mein,
Vaisakh Maah Wali II Om Jai Ekadashi... II
Shukla Paksh Mein Hoy Mohini Apara
Jyeshtha Krishna Pakshi,
Naam Nirjala Sab Sukh Karni,
Shukla Paksh Rakhi II Om Jai Ekadashi... II
Yogini Naam Aashadh Mein Jaano,
Krishna Paksh Karni,
Devshayani Naam Kahaayo,
Shukla Paksh Dharni II Om Jai Ekadashi... II
Kaamika Shraavan Maas Mein Aavai,
Krishna Paksh Kahiye,
Shraavan Shukla Hoy Pavitra Anand Se
Rahiye II Om Jai Ekadashi... II
Ajaa Bhadrapad Krishnapaksh Ki,
Parivartini Shukla I
Indra Aashchin Krishnapaksh Mein,
Vrat Se Bhavasagar Nikla II
Om Jai Ekadashi... II
Paapankusha Hai Shukla Paksh Mein,
Aap Haranhari I
Rama Maas Kartik Mein Aavai,
Sukhadayak Bhaari II Om Jai Ekadashi... II
Devotthani Shuklapaksh Ki,

Dukhanashak Maiyaa I
Paavan Maas Mein Karoon Vinati
Paar Karo Naiyaa II Om Jai Ekadashi... II
Parmaa Krishnapaksh Mein Hoti,
Jan Mangal Karni I
Shukla Maas Mein Hoy Padmini Dukh
Daridra Harni II Om Jai Ekadashi... II
Jo Koi Aarti Ekadashi Ki,
Bhakti Sahit Gaavai I
Jan Gurdita Swarg Ka Vasa,
Nishchay Vah Paavai II Om Jai Ekadashi... II

॥ Shri Tulsi Ji Ki Aarti ॥

Jai Jai Tulsi Mata,
Sabki Sukhdata Var Mata I
Sab Yogon Ke Upar,
Sab Rogon Ke Upar,
Ruj Se Raksha Karke Bhav Trata I
Jai Jai Tulsi Mata I
Bahut Putri Hai Shyama,
Soor Valli Hai Gramya,
Vishnu Priya Jo Tumko Seve,
So Nar Tar Jata I
Jai Jai Tulsi Mata I
Hari Ke Sheesh Virajat
Tribhuvan Se Ho Vandit,
Patit Jano Ki Tarini,
Tum Ho Vikhyata I
Jai Jai Tulsi Mata I
Lekar Janm Bijan Mein
Aayi DivyaBhavan Mein,
Manav Lok Tumhi Se
Sukh Sampatti Pata I
Jai Jai Tulsi Mata I
Hari Ko Tum Ati Pyari
Shyam Varn Sukumari,
Prem Ajab Hai
Shri Hari Ka Tum Se Nata I
Jai Jai Tulsi Mata I

II Jai Jai Gayatri Mata II

Jaiti Jai Gayatri Mata,
Jaiti Jai Gayatri Mata I
Sat Marg Par Humein Chalao,
Jo Hai Sukhdata II

Jaiti Jai Gayatri Mata... I
Adi Shakti Tum Alakh Niranjan,
Jag Palan Kartri I
Dukh, Shok, Bhay, Klesh,
Kalah, Daridry, Dainy Hartri II

Jaiti Jai Gayatri Mata... I
Brahma Rupini, Pranat Palini,
Jagatdhatri Ambe I
Bhavbhayahari, Janhitkari,
Sukhda Jagdambe II

Jaiti Jai Gayatri Mata... I
Bhayharini Bhavtarini, Anaghe,
Aj Anand Rashi I
Avikari, Aghahari, Avichalit,
Amale, Avinashi II

Jaiti Jai Gayatri Mata... I

Kamdhenu Sat Chit Ananda,
Jai Ganga Geeta I
Savita Ki Shashwati Shakti,
Tum Savitri Sita II

Jaiti Jai Gayatri Mata... I
Rig, Yaju, Sam, Atharv,
Pranayini, Pranav Mahamhime I
Kundalini Sahasrar, Sushumna,
Shobha Gun Garime II

Jaiti Jai Gayatri Mata... I
Swaha, Swadha, Shachi,
Brahani, Radha, Rudrani I
Jai Satarupa, Vani, Vidya, Kamla,
Kalyani II

Jaiti Jai Gayatri Mata... I
Janani Hum Hai, Deen, Heen,
Dukh, Daridr Ke Ghere I
Yadapi Kutil, Kapti, Kaput,
Tau Balak Hai Tere II

Jaiti Jai Gay

ll Aarti Shri Gayatri Ji Ki ll

Aarti Shri Gayatri Ji Ki l
Gyanadeep aur shraddha ki baati l
So bhakti hi poorti karai jahan ghee ki ll
Aarti Shri Gayatri Ji Ki l
Maanas ki shuchi thaal ke upar l
Devi ki jyot jagai, jahan neeki ll
Aarti Shri Gayatri Ji Ki l
Shuddh manorath te jahan ghanta l
Baajai karai asuhi hi ki ll
Aarti Shri Gayatri Ji Ki l
Jaake samaksh humein tihun lok kai l
Gaddi milai sabhun lagai feeki ll
Aarti Shri Gayatri Ji Ki l
Sankat aavai na paas kabou tinhen l
Sampada aur sukh ki banai leeki ll
Aarti Shri Gayatri Ji Ki l
Aarti prem sau nem so kari l
Dhyaavahin murti Brahm lali ki ll
Aarti Shri Gayatri Ji Ki l

II Shri Sheetla Mata Ki Aarti II

Jai Sheetla Mata,
Maiya Jai Sheetla Mata I
Aadi Jyoti Maharani
Sab Phal Ki Data II
Om Jai Sheetla Mata... I
Ratan Singhasan Shobhit,
Shwet Chhatra Bhata I
Riddhi-Siddhi Chanvar Dolavein,
Jagmag Chhavi Chhata II
Om Jai Sheetla Mata... I
Vishnu Sevat Thadhe,
Seve Shiv Dhata I
Ved Puran Varanat Paar Nahin Paata II
Om Jai Sheetla Mata... I
Indra Mridang Bajavat,
Chandra Veena Haatha I
Suraj Taal Bajavai Narad Muni Gata II
Om Jai Sheetla Mata... I
Ghanta Shankh Shehnai
Bajai Man Bhata I
Karai Bhakt Jan Aarti
Lakhi Lakhi Harshata II
Om Jai Sheetla Mata... I

Brahma Roop Varadani
Tuhi Teen Kaal Gyata I
Bhaktan Ko Sukh Deti
Maatu Pita Bhrata II
Om Jai Sheetla Mata... I
Jo Jan Dhyan Lagave
Prem Shakti Pata I
Sakal Manorath Pave
Bhavanidhi Tar Jata II
Om Jai Sheetla Mata... I
Rogon Se Jo Peedit Koi
Sharan Teri Aata I
Kodhi Pave Nirmal Kaya
Andh Netra Pata II
Om Jai Sheetla Mata... I
Baanjh Putra Ko Pave Daridr Kat Jata I
Tako Bhajai Jo Nahin Sir Dhuni Pachtata II
Om Jai Sheetla Mata... I
Sheetal Karti Jan Ki Tu Hi Hai Jag Trata I
Utpatti Bala Binashan Tu Sab Ki Mata II
Om Jai Sheetla Mata... I
Daas Narayan Kar Jori Mata I
Bhakti Apni Dijiye Aur Na Kuchh Mata II
Om Jai Sheetla Mata... I

II Shri Gaumataji Ki Aarti II

Aarti Shri Gaiyya Maiyya Ki,
Aarti Harni Vishva Dhaiyya Ki I
Aarti Shri Gaiyya Maiyya Ki... I

Arthkaam Saddharma Pradayani,
Avichal Amal Muktipaddayini I
Sur Manav Saubhagya Vidhayani,
Pyari Poojya Nand Chhaiyya Ki II

Aarti Shri Gaiyya Maiyya Ki... I

Akhil Vishva Pratipalini Mata,
Madhur Amiya Dugdhanna Pradata I
Rog Shok Sankat Paritrata,
Bhavasagar Hit Dridha Naiyya Ki II

Aarti Shri Gaiyya Maiyya Ki... I

Ayu Oj Arogya Vikashini,
Dukh Dainya Daridrya Vinashini I

Sushma Saukhya Samriddhi
Prakashini,
Vimal Vivek Buddhi Daiyya Ki II

Aarti Shri Gaiyya Maiyya Ki... I

Sevak Ho Chahe Dukhdai,
Sam Pay Sudha Piyavati Mai I
Shatru-Mitra Sabko Sukhdayi,
Sneh Swabhav Vishva Jaiyya Ki II

Aarti Shri Gaiyya Maiyya Ki... I
Aarti Shri Gaiyya Maiyya Ki,
Aarti Harni Vishva Dhaiyya Ki I

Aarti Shri Gaiyya Maiyya Ki... I

II Shri Radha Mata Ji Ki Aarti II

Aarti Shri Vrishbhanusuta Ki,
Manjul Murti Mohan Mamta Ki I
Trividha Tapayut Sansriti Nashini,
Vimal Vivekviraag Vikasini I
Pavan Prabhu Pad Preeti Prakashini,
Sundartam Chhavi Sundarta Ki II

Aarti Shri Vrishbhanusuta Ki I
Muni Man Mohan Mohan Mohani,
Madhur Manohar Murti Sohani I
Aviralprem Amiya Ras Dohani,
Priya Ati Sada Sakhi Lalita Ki II

Aarti Shri Vrishbhanusuta Ki I
Santat Sevya Sat Muni Janki,
Aakar Amit Divyagun Ganki I
Aakarshini Krishna Tan Man Ki,
Ati Amulya Sampati Samta Ki II

Aarti Shri Vrishbhanusuta Ki I
Krishnatmika Krishna Sahcharini,
Chinmayavrinda Vipin Viharini I
Jagajjanani Jag Dukh Nivarini,
Adi Anadi Shakti Vibhuta Ki II

Aarti Shri Vrishbhanusuta Ki II

II Shri Shakambhari Mata Ji Ki Aarti II

Hari Om

Shri Shakambhar Amba Ji KiAarti Kijo I

Aiso Adbhut Roop Hriday Dhar Liejo,

Shatakshi Dayalu Ki Aarti Kijo I

Tum Paripurn Adi Bhavani Maa,

Sab Ghat Tum Aap Bakhani Maa I

Shri Shakambhar Amba Ji Ki Aarti Kijo I

Tumhi Ho Shakambhari,

Tum Hi Ho Shatakshi Maa I

Shiv Murti Maya,

Tum Hi Ho Prakashi Maa I

Shri Shakambhar Amba Ji Ki Aarti Kijo I

Nit Jo Nar-Nari,
Ambe Aarti Gave Maa,
Iccha Pooran Kijo,
Shakambhari Darshan Pave Maa I

Shri Shakambhar Amba Ji Ki Aarti Kijo I

Jo Nar Aarti Padhe Padhave Maa,
Jo Nar Aarti Sune Sunave Maa I Base

Vaikunth Shakambhar Darshan Pave I

Shri Shakambhar Amba Ji Ki Aarti Kijo I

Maiya Sharda Tore Darbar
Aarti Nit Gaun I x3
Tap Ko Haar Karn Ko Teeka
Dhyan Ki Dhwaja Chadhaun I x2
Darsh Tore Paun I
Maiya Sharda Tore Darbar
Aarti Nit Gaun I x3
Maa Ke Bhajan Sadhu Santan Ko
Aarti Roj Sunau I x2
Darsh Tore Paun I
Maiya Sharda Tore Darbar
Aarti Nit Gaun I x3
Sumar-Sumar Maa Ke Jas Gawe
Charnan Sheesh Navaun I x2
Darsh Tore Paun I
Maiya Sharda Tore Darbar
Aarti Nit Gaun I x3
Maiya Sharda Tore Darbar
Aarti Nit Gaun I x2
Maiya Sharda Tore Darbar
Aarti Nit Gaun I x3

Sri Navgrah Aarti

Aarti Shri Navagrahon Ki Kijiye,
Badha, Kasht, Rog Har Lijiye।

Surya Tej Vyaap Bhar,
Jaki Kripa Kaabahu Nahi Chhijiye॥
Aarti Shri Navagrahon Ki Kijiye॥

Roop Chandra Sheetalta Laaye,
Shanti Sahit Saras Rasu Bhayo।
Aarti Shri Navagrahon Ki Kijiye॥

Mangal Hare Amangal Mangal Saara,
Saumya Sudha Ras Amrit Pije।
Aarti Shri Navagrahon Ki Kijiye॥

Buddh Sada Vaibhav Yash Liye,
Sukh Sampatti Lakshmi Pasije।
Aarti Shri Navagrahon Ki Kijiye॥

Vidya Buddh Gyaan Guru Se Le Lo,
Pragati Sada Manav Pe Rejhe।

Aarti Shri Navagrahon Ki Kijiye ll

Shukra Tark Vigyan Badhave,
Desh Dharma Seva Yash Lije l
Aarti Shri Navagrahon Ki Kijiye ll

Nyaykari Shani Atyant Nyare,
Jap Tap Shraddha Shani Ko Dijiye l
Aarti Shri Navagrahon Ki Kijiye ll

Rahu Man Ka Bharam Harave,
Saath Na Kabhu Kukarm Na Dijiye l
Aarti Shri Navagrahon Ki Kijiye ll

Swasthya Uttam Ketu Rakhe,
Paradhinta Manhit Khije l
Aarti Shri Navagrahon Ki Kijiye ll

9 789334 371130

Printed at Repro India Ltd.